200 fast family favourites

hamlyn | all colour cookbook

200 fast family favourites

An Hachette UK Company
www.hachette.co.uk

First published in Great Britain in 2010 by
Hamlyn, a division of Octopus Publishing Group Ltd
Endeavour House
189 Shaftesbury Avenue
London
WC2H 8JY
www.octopusbooks.co.uk

ISBN 978-0-600-62148-5

A CIP catalogue record for this book is available from
the British Library.

Printed and bound in China

10 9 8 7 6 5 4 3 2 1

Both metric and imperial measurements have
been given in all recipes. Use one set of measurements
only, and not a mixture of both.

Standard level spoon measurements are used in all recipes.
1 tablespoon = one 15 ml spoon
1 teaspoon = one 5 ml spoon

Ovens should be preheated to the specified temperature
– if using a fan-assisted oven, follow the manufacturer's
instructions for adjusting the time and the temperature.

Fresh herbs should be used unless otherwise stated.

Medium eggs should be used unless otherwise stated.

The Department of Health advises that eggs should not be
consumed raw. This book contains some dishes made with
raw or lightly cooked eggs. It is prudent for vulnerable people
such as pregnant and nursing mothers, invalids, the elderly,
babies and young children to avoid uncooked or lightly
cooked dishes made with eggs. Once prepared, these dishes
should be kept refrigerated and used promptly.

This book includes dishes made with nuts and nut derivatives.
It is advisable for those with known allergic reactions to nuts
and nut derivatives and those who may be potentially
vulnerable to these allergies, such as pregnant and nursing
mothers, invalids, the elderly, babies and children, to avoid
dishes made with nuts and nut oils. It is also prudent to check
the labels of pre-prepared ingredients for the possible
inclusion of nut derivatives.

contents

introduction

introduction

These days, most families' lives are packed with activity. Not only do many parents have to juggle their work with child care, but their spare time is increasingly taken up with activities that fulfil their own and their children's physical, creative and social needs. Children, too, have busy and varied lives. Even after school it's likely that the rest of the day will be a busy round of being dropped off at ballet class or gym club or football training or being collected from swimming classes or drum or judo practice. Then there's barely time to get everybody fed and the young ones into bed before it's time for the adults to go off to band practice or simply to put up their feet and have a quiet glass of wine.

When we stop to think about our modern lives, it's easy to see how meals can get pushed into the background and be made to fit around our other commitments. Time is in such short supply that most of us scarcely have time to eat our meals, let alone plan them, shop for them and cook them. That is why we have included the recipes in this book, which bring together some delicious and nutritious dishes that all the family can enjoy together and that will only take a short time to prepare and cook. When you spend less time in the kitchen, you will have more time to savour and enjoy both your food and the company of your family and friends.

the benefits of family meals

Many of us are guilty of grabbing supper as we are on the way to a meeting, or we let the children perch on stools at the kitchen worktop to wolf down a bowl of something hot before they set off to do something else.

But we should all remember the huge benefits that accrue to both ourselves and our children if we sit down together as a family around the dining table to eat a proper meal. This is not only important from the nutritional point of view, but is also a major part of growing up and one that most of us can remember from our own childhoods.

Mealtimes should be significant social events for families. They give an opportunity for us to talk to each other about what has happened during the day without the sound of a television set in the background distracting our attention. They also give us a chance to be good role models for our children. Eating together enables us to encourage the children to try out new foods as well as making sure that they have healthier versions of the foods they love. Sitting down to eat a meal in a structured, sensitive and loving environment also gives children an opportunity to learn good table manners – something we all hope and assume they will learn by the time they reach adulthood.

In addition, when you eat meals sitting down at a table, your body will be able to get more nutrients from the food you are eating. So switch off the television and lay the table.

being prepared

Although most people recognize the benefits of providing well-cooked and well-presented meals, they often fail in the preparation of family meals. You may have great plans for a sit-down meal, but if it takes a long time to prepare, the time you spend eating and enjoying it is minimal and undermines your good intentions. So we have come up with this selection of quick and easy recipes. Some of these dishes are already well-known family favourites, but others we hope will become new regulars in your family. Not only are they all quick to prepare, but they are also highly nutritious and taste wonderful.

The key to a successful family meal lies in the planning. If you know you have a busy week ahead, try and find time to sit down the week before and plan your meals and draw up a shopping list. If time is really tight, consider using online shopping services. Although there is a delivery fee, you will save a huge amount of time when you don't have to walk around the supermarket and handle the products yourself. All you have to do is transfer the shopping to your cupboards when it's been delivered. Internet food shopping can save you hours each month.

key ingredients

Even when you have spent time making plans, sometimes things change at the last minute, and you may find that you have no time at all to prepare something from scratch. For this reason it's a good idea to keep a few key

ingredients in your cupboards just for such emergencies.

There are some basic foodstuffs that you will always need. These include staple carbohydrates, such as rice and pasta (ideally brown if you can buy it), couscous, noodles and porridge oats. Even when you have no fresh meat, if you have a bag of cashew nuts and a store of canned tuna, salmon and beans in the cupboard, some eggs in the refrigerator and a bag of frozen prawns in the freezer you can still provide a nutritious protein-based dinner in a matter of minutes.

To add flavour and to help the cooking process, make sure you always have some chicken and vegetable stock cubes or granules and soy sauce, together with olive,

sesame and rapeseed oils, salt and pepper and tomato and sun-dried tomato paste. You should also have some key herbs and spices, such as mixed herbs, mixed spice, Chinese five-spice powder, ground cinnamon, coriander, cumin and nutmeg and chilli sauce or flakes.

Other produce you should keep to help you create some last-minute sauces include flour, cornflour, canned tomatoes, passata, olives, mature Cheddar cheese and some UHT dried milk. And for emergency desserts keep sugar, honey, maple syrup, a couple of cans of tinned fruit and some digestive biscuits in the cupboard and some vanilla ice cream, fruit sorbet and waffles in the freezer.

Crème fraîche and plain yogurt can be used in both savoury and sweet dishes, but these ingredients have a short shelf life and should ideally be bought during your regular shopping trips.

Although it's not a good idea to rely on ready-made sauces, which are often made with unnecessary preservatives and colourings, it is useful to have a jar or two of good-quality green or red pesto in your cupboard. You can spread a little pesto over baked chicken or fish or stir it through pasta for a quick and delicious lunch. The best-quality pesto is made only with basil, Parmesan cheese, pine nuts and olive oil, and it's easy to make in a food processor from scratch yourself, but when time is limited a good ready-made version is one of the best 'chef's cheats' you can buy.

short cuts

With a great selection of basic ingredients in your kitchen cupboards, a little time spent planning your weekly meals and your shopping delivered to your door, you are nearly ready to get down to feeding your hungry family this week. But before you do so, try and fit in a few small jobs the next time you find yourself with some spare minutes. They will save time later and help take some of the fiddle out of preparing good-quality, nutritious meals.

When bread starts to go stale, don't throw it away or put it on the compost. Instead, put it in the food processor and make breadcrumbs. Bag them up and store them in the freezer for the next time you're making breaded chicken nuggets or need a crunchy topping for an oven-bake.

Grate Cheddar and Parmesan cheese and freeze them in small portions ready for use in sauces and risottos. Keep ginger and chillies in your freezer. You can grate ginger when it's still frozen straight into your recipe. Chillies need a few minutes to thaw before they are ready for chopping. Buy ready-chopped frozen spinach, which can be added to dishes straight from the freezer.

When you make a soup, stew, curry or ragout-style sauce, make double the quantity specified in the recipe and store the surplus in your freezer. When you need to create an emergency meal, it is amazing what you will be able to find in your freezer to save the day.

If you do not have a microwave and have forgotten to take meat, poultry or fish out of the freezer, you can speed up the process of defrosting by immersing the wrapped frozen food in a sink of cold water and leaving it for a couple of hours.

Instead of crushing garlic, chop the end off a clove and grate it instead. It saves time washing up the garlic crusher and wastes less of the clove. If the recipe requires a large number of garlic cloves, you can save time by adding garlic paste straight from the tube. The flavour is intense, so take care: you need only a small amount to replace a clove of garlic.

If you have some double cream left, pour it into ice-cube trays and freeze it. You can then remove as little or as much as you need for the next recipe that requires it.

Fresh coriander is a wonderful herb, which adds huge amounts of flavour to all sorts of dishes. Make sure you always have the flavour of 'fresh coriander' by keeping a store of pots or tubes of coriander paste, which preserves the coriander leaves in a mixture of oil and vinegar. Alternatively, freeze a bunch of fresh coriander in a polythene bag ready to crumble into your cooking. Freezing will blacken the leaves and marginally reduce the fresh coriander at all.

Pre-slice bread before you freeze it. You can then remove only the amount you actually require. Similarly, cut muffins in half before freezing them so you can take them straight from the freezer and put them under the grill for toasting.

fast food that's good food

Whether you are young or old, a vegetarian or an omnivore, we all need much the same nutrients from the food we eat. Our energy comes from food and fluids, and if we are to get the full and complete range of nutrients that our bodies need we should be consuming carbohydrates, protein, fats, fibre and water as

well as a variety of vitamins and minerals. These nutrients not only fuel our bodies, but many of them also actually improve our health and help protect us against diseases. If we eat well, we feel well, our mood is improved, and we can cope better with stress – which can only be a good thing if we're running a busy household.

Just because time is limited does not mean that we can't eat healthily. Fast food can still be good, nutritious and healthy food, as many of the recipes in this book prove. The secret is to mix up the dishes and get the family eating as great a variety of foods as possible, so that everyone gets all the nutrition they need and a chance to eat their favourite food at some point in the week. If one child hates beans but loves red meat, while the other hates red meat but loves omelettes, so be it. You may not be able to please the whole family in one sitting, but if you mix up the recipes everyone will have at least one meal a week that they really love, and you will avoid falling into a 'meal rut', when you eat the same foods day after day.

In the second chapter of this book, Pasta, Rice and Noodles, the recipes are based on a range of carbohydrates. Although carbs have had a bad press in recent years, good carbohydrates (otherwise known as complex carbohydrates) are actually vital to our health and should form the basis of every healthy diet. Complex carbohydrates include grains, bread, rice and pasta as well as fresh fruits and vegetables, pulses and dairy products.

Fresh fruits and vegetables are not every child's favourite food, but they should form the basis of every meal and should also, ideally, be your first choice for snacks. They are packed with antioxidants, which protect us against disease, and contain vitamins and minerals, such as iron and calcium, to make our bodies work properly. For this reason, fruits and vegetables feature in many of the recipes in this book. They will add important vitamins and minerals to your diet and give your food a great flavour and colour. Pasta, rice and noodles are firm favourites in the Western diet, and this isn't surprising because they are a great base to which can be added a host of intoxicating flavours. Whenever you can, choose brown or wholemeal versions because the nutrients have not been processed out of them and they retain their fibre content.

Fibre is found only in plant-based foods, and it is vital for the health of the whole family. First, fibre keeps the gut healthy and aids digestion, and second, fibrous foods help to maintain our blood-sugar levels. Fibre takes longer to digest than other types of foods, helping to make you feel fuller for longer, which helps overcome the temptation of snacking on unhealthy, fatty foods in between meals.

Pulses are another good source of fibre, and they feature in several tasty dishes in the One Pot and Vegetarian chapters. Persuading your family to eat pulses will benefit everybody. They are a good source of protein, are full of B vitamins, calcium and iron, are low in saturated fat and are cholesterol free. Teenage girls especially, who often go through phases of faddy eating or experiment with vegetarianism, have an increased need for iron and will benefit if there are more pulses in their diet. Let them try Braised Lentils with Gremolata (see pages 196–7) or Chorizo and Chickpea Stew (see pages 138–9). Or you could spoil the whole family by cooking the Sausage and Bean Casserole (see pages 88–9), which is real comfort food for a wintry day.

encouraging fussy eaters

Children young and old can be notoriously fussy eaters, and many seem to be able to exist on pasta, sandwiches and little else. But if you want your children to develop healthy eating habits and you are keen to cook and share family meals together, it is vital that your children learn to like and accept new and different tastes. Cooking twice in one evening, once for the children and once for the adults, not only is exhausting, but also allows the children to develop picky and fussy eating habits, as they are able to demand their favourites night after night.

If your children are typical, getting them to eat protein probably won't be a problem. Many of the Meaty Treats in the fourth chapter are real family classics, and few children (or adults) will be able to resist Sausages with Mustard Mash (see pages 116–17). Sweet and Sour Pork (see pages 132–3) is an absolute winner with adults and children alike.

Getting younger children to eat fish and seafood can be more difficult, but try Roast Cod and Olive Risotto (see pages 164–5) or Monkfish Kebabs (see pages 170–71), and you will be pleasantly surprised to see the whole family wolf down their fish and ask for more.

trying new foods

When you cook for the whole family so that everyone eats together you will start to encourage your children to try new tastes and textures. Start simply. Suggest to the family that one day in the week is the day to try new foods – 'Trying Tuesdays', for example – and reward younger children who eat something new with a sticker or star chart. Older children can be allowed to stay up for 10 minutes later in the evening.

Present the meal in serving bowls and encourage children to help themselves. This will help them feel they have some control over what is put on their plates, and they will be more inclined to eat it. Do not bribe children with food, and never force a child to eat something they clearly don't like. A bad experience at the dinner table will stay in a child's memory for a long time, and they will associate negative feelings with that food for months or even years afterwards.

On days when you are offering new foods, avoid snacks close to dinner time so that everyone will be hungry before their meal. If you do this there is a greater chance that fussy eaters will eat whatever is presented to them. If a child continually refuses their food, make sure that they are not drinking too much fruit juice or are snacking between meals, both of which can take away the appetite.

Never prepare an alternative if a child refuses the meal that you have cooked for them. This only encourages fussy behaviour and will slowly erode your enjoyment of cooking for your family.

Be aware that children have sensitive taste buds, so be cautious when you are adding exotic and spicy flavours. When you are preparing a curry, for example, it may be wise to let your children get used to the more exotic flavours within the meal before adding any chilli.

eating together

Remember that when a family eats together you have an opportunity to be a wonderful role model for your children. If you love curry, they will secretly want to like curry too, so keep cooking new dishes and keep offering young children lots of encouragement. In time, by making mealtimes fun, interesting and happy social events, you will discover that your children will happily eat all sorts of different flavours, textures and dishes, and you will regularly be able to enjoy good, healthy food together as a family.

So get cooking and start creating some wonderful mealtime memories.

snacks & light bites

minestrone soup

Serves **4**
Preparation time **5 minutes**
Cooking time **25 minutes**

2 tablespoons **olive oil**
1 **onion**, diced
1 **garlic clove**, crushed
2 **celery sticks**, chopped
1 **leek**, finely sliced
1 **carrot**, chopped
400 g (13 oz) can **chopped
  tomatoes**
600 ml (1 pint) **chicken stock**
  or **vegetable stock**
1 **courgette**, diced
½ small **green cabbage**,
  shredded
1 **bay leaf**
75 g (3 oz) canned **haricot
  beans**
75 g (3 oz) **spaghetti**, broken
  into small pieces, or small
  pasta shapes
1 tablespoon chopped **flat
  leaf parsley**
salt and **pepper**
50 g (2 oz) **Parmesan
  cheese**, freshly grated,
  to serve

Heat the oil in a large saucepan. Add the onion, garlic, celery, leek and carrot and sauté over a medium heat, stirring occasionally, for 3 minutes.

Add the tomatoes, stock, courgette, cabbage, bay leaf and haricot beans. Bring to the boil, then lower the heat and simmer for 10 minutes.

Add the spaghetti and season to taste with salt and pepper. Stir well and cook for a further 8 minutes. Keep stirring, otherwise the soup may stick to the base of the pan.

Add the chopped parsley just before serving, and stir well. Ladle into warm soup bowls and serve with grated Parmesan.

For bacon & lentil soup, fry 6 rashers roughly chopped streaky bacon with the onion, garlic and vegetables and then add 75 g (3 oz) red lentils with the tomatoes, stock and haricot beans. Simmer for 20 minutes until the lentils make the soup thicken naturally. Omit the pasta. Serve in warm serving bowls with 1 tablespoon chopped parsley stirred through and 50 g (2 oz) grated Parmesan cheese sprinkled over.

summer vegetable soup

Serves **4**
Preparation time **10 minutes**
Cooking time **20 minutes**

1 teaspoon **olive oil**
1 **leek**, thinly sliced
1 large **potato**, chopped
450 g (14½ oz) prepared
   mixed summer vegetables,
   such as peas, asparagus
   spears, broad beans and
   courgettes
2 tablespoons chopped **mint**,
   plus extra leaves to garnish
900 ml (1½ pints) **vegetable
   stock**
2 tablespoons **crème fraîche**
salt (optional) and **pepper**

Heat the oil in a medium saucepan, add the leek and potato and cook for 3–4 minutes until softened.

Add the mixed vegetables to the pan with the mint and stock and bring to the boil. Reduce the heat and simmer for 10 minutes.

Transfer the soup to a blender or food processor and blend until smooth. Return the soup to the pan and season to taste with salt, if necessary, and pepper. Heat through and serve in warmed bowls with the crème fraîche swirled over the top. Garnish with extra mint leaves.

For vegetable soup with cheesy croûtons, cook 1 leek and 1 large potato as above, add 900 ml (1½ pints) vegetable stock and bring to the boil. Cook for 10 minutes, then transfer to a food processor or blender and process until smooth. Return to the pan and add a further 150 ml (¼ pint) stock, all the remaining vegetables, roughly chopped, and 2 tablespoons chopped mint. Cook for a further 10 minutes. Meanwhile, thinly slice a thin French baguette, cover the slices with grated Cheddar cheese and grill under a preheated hot grill for 5 minutes until golden and bubbling. Serve the soup in warm serving bowls with the cheesy toast on top.

chicken noodle soup

Serves **4**
Preparation time **10 minutes**
Cooking time **12 minutes**

1.2 litres (2 pints) **chicken stock**
1 **star anise**
7 cm (3 inch) piece of **cinnamon stick**, broken up
2 **garlic cloves**, finely chopped
2 tablespoons **Thai fish sauce**
8 **coriander roots**, finely chopped
4 teaspoons **light soft brown sugar**
4 teaspoons **light soy sauce**
200 g (7 oz) boneless, skinless **chicken breast**, cut into cubes
125 g (4 oz) **green vegetables**, such as spring cabbage, chard or pak choi, roughly chopped
75 g (3 oz) **bean sprouts**
200 g (7 oz) **straight to wok rice noodles**
15 g (½ oz) fresh **coriander leaves**

Put the chicken stock, star anise, cinnamon stick, garlic, fish sauce, coriander, sugar and soy sauce into a large saucepan and bring slowly to the boil.

Add the chicken and simmer gently for 4 minutes.

Add the green vegetables and bean sprouts and simmer for 2 minutes.

Divide the noodles between 4 bowls, pour over the soup and sprinkle the coriander on top.

For coconut & chicken soup, replace 400 ml (14 fl oz) of the chicken stock with 400 ml (14 fl oz) canned coconut milk (either half-fat or full-fat). Cook the stock, herbs and spices, sugar and fish and soy sauces, and chicken as above, simmering the green vegetables and bean sprouts for 2 minutes and adding 125 g (4 oz) shredded mangetout for the final 1 minute of cooking for extra crunch. Ladle into warm serving bowls over noodles as above and garnish with fresh coriander leaves.

croque monsieur

Serves **4**
Preparation time **10 minutes**
Cooking time **10 minutes**

100 g (3½ oz) **butter**,
  softened
8 slices of **white bread**
4 slices of **Cheddar cheese**
4 slices of cooked **ham**
4 tablespoons **vegetable oil**
pepper

Spread half the butter over one side of each slice of bread. Put a slice of Cheddar on 4 of the buttered slices, top with a slice of ham and sprinkle with pepper. Top with the remaining slices of bread, butter side down, and press down hard.

Melt half the rest of the butter with half the oil in a large frying pan, and fry 2 croques until golden brown, turning once. Cook the remaining 2 in the same way.

For croque madames, prepare the croque monsieurs as above but omit the cheese. Heat 4 tablespoons vegetable oil in a frying pan and cook the ham sandwiches until they are golden and warm. Remove from the pan and keep warm. Add a further 1 tablespoon oil to the pan and break 4 eggs into the pan. Cook until the white is firm but the yolk is still soft. Transfer the warm ham sandwiches to warm serving plates and use a fish slice to lay an egg on top of each. Garnish with chopped flat leaf parsley to serve.

homemade sausage rolls

Makes **15**
Preparation time **15 minutes**,
 plus chilling
Cooking time **15 minutes**

400 g (13 oz) good-quality
 sausages
200 g (7 oz) **plain flour**, plus
 extra for dusting
50 g (2 oz) **wholemeal flour**
pinch of **salt**
150 g (5 oz) **butter**, chilled
 and diced
3 tablespoons **iced water**
1 tablespoon **poppy seeds**
1 **egg**, beaten

Snip each sausage at one end and squeeze the sausage meat out on to a chopping board lightly dusted with flour. Roll out into thinner sausages.

Sift both flours and the salt into a bowl. Add the butter and rub it in with the fingertips until the mixture resembles fine breadcrumbs. Add enough of the measurement iced water to mix to a soft dough, then stir in the poppy seeds. Turn the dough out on to a lightly floured surface and knead briefly.

Roll the pastry out on a well-floured surface to a rectangle measuring 30 x 25 cm (12 x 10 inches), then cut into three 10 x 25 cm (4 x 10 inch) strips. Lay the sausage meat down the centre of each strip. Brush 1 edge of each strip with beaten egg, roll over and flute the edges. Cut each strip into five 5 cm (2 inch) sausage rolls and put on a baking sheet.

Make a couple of cuts in the top of each roll and brush with the remaining egg. Refrigerate for 15 minutes before baking in a preheated oven, 200°C (400°F), Gas Mark 6, for 15 minutes. Remove from the oven and leave to cool before lifting off the sheet.

For roasted vegetable & sausage rolls, core, deseed and roughly chop 1 small red and 1 small yellow pepper and chop 1 medium courgette. Toss the vegetables with 1 tablespoon olive oil and roast on a baking sheet in a preheated oven, 200°C (400°F), Gas Mark 6, for 30 minutes until softened. Allow to cool. Combine the vegetables with 300 g (10 oz) sausage meat. Roll out the pastry, then use the stuffing to make 15 sausage rolls. Bake as above.

goats' cheese omelettes

Serves **4**
Preparation time **10 minutes**
Cooking time **20 minutes**

4 tablespoons **olive oil**
500 g (1 lb) **cherry tomatoes**
 (mixed red and yellow),
 halved
a little chopped **basil**
12 **eggs**
2 tablespoons **wholegrain**
 mustard
50 g (2 oz) **butter**
100 g (3½ oz) **soft goats'**
 cheese, diced
salt and **pepper**
watercress, to garnish

Heat the oil in a frying pan and fry the tomatoes (you may have to do this in 2 batches) for 2–3 minutes until they have softened. Add the basil and season with salt and pepper, then transfer to a bowl and keep warm.

Beat the eggs with the mustard and season with salt and pepper.

Melt a quarter of the butter in an omelette pan or small frying pan until it stops foaming, then swirl in a quarter of the egg mixture. Fork over the omelette so that it cooks evenly. As soon as it is set on the bottom (but still a little runny in the middle), dot over a quarter of the goats' cheese and cook for a further 30 seconds. Carefully slide the omelette on to a warmed plate, folding it in half as you do so.

Repeat with the remaining mixture to make 3 more omelettes. Serve with the tomatoes and garnish with watercress.

For chorizo, plum tomato & chilli omelettes, cut 6 large plum tomatoes into quarters and fry them in 4 tablespoons olive oil. Add 225 g (7½ oz) thinly sliced chorizo sausage and 1 teaspoon chopped fresh chilli. Cook for a further minute until lightly browned. Beat and cook the eggs as above, but omit the goats' cheese. Serve the omelettes with the chorizo mixture, garnished with rocket leaves.

blt sandwich

Serves **1**
Preparation time **5 minutes**
Cooking time **10 minutes**

2 lean **bacon** rashers
2 slices of **wholemeal bread**
  or **multi-grain bread**
2 tablespoons **mayonnaise**
2 **tomatoes**, halved
about 4 **baby lettuce leaves**
salt and **pepper**

Heat a small, nonstick frying pan and cook the bacon, turning once, until it is golden brown and crisp. Remove and drain on kitchen paper.

Toast the bread on both sides. Spread one side of each piece of toast with mayonnaise and arrange the bacon, tomatoes and lettuce on top of one of the pieces. Season with salt and pepper and top with the other piece of toast. Cut into quarters. Serve hot or cold.

For a toasted breakfast sandwich, cook the bacon as above. Cook 2 thick pork sausages until golden and cooked through. Slice the sausages lengthways into 3 long thin slices and set aside to keep warm. In a separate, medium-sized frying pan heat 1 tablespoon vegetable oil. Beat 2 eggs and cook over a moderate heat for 1–2 minutes until just set. Arrange the bacon and sausages on a slice of warm toast. Cut the egg into quarters and arrange on top. Season with pepper and scatter over chopped parsley. Spread a little ketchup or brown sauce on the other slice of toast and top the sandwich. Cut into quarters and serve warm.

chicken dippers with salsa

Serves **4**
Preparation time **20 minutes**
Cooking time **6–8 minutes**

2 **eggs**
2 tablespoons **milk**
100 g (3½ oz) **fresh breadcrumbs**
4 tablespoons freshly grated **Parmesan cheese**
3 boneless, skinless **chicken breasts**, about 500 g (1 lb) in total, cut into long, finger-like slices
25 g (1 oz) **butter**
2 tablespoons **vegetable oil**
salt and **pepper**

Salsa
2 **tomatoes**, diced
¼ **cucumber**, diced
75 g (3 oz) **sweetcorn**, defrosted if frozen
1 tablespoon fresh **coriander leaves**, chopped

Put the salsa ingredients in a bowl and mix together.

Beat the eggs, milk and a little salt and pepper together in a bowl.

Mix the breadcrumbs with the Parmesan.

Dip one chicken strip into the egg, then roll in the breadcrumbs. Carry on doing this until all the chicken strips are well covered.

Heat the butter and oil in a large frying pan and add the chicken strips. Cook for 6–8 minutes, turning a few times until they are brown all over. Serve with the salsa to dip into.

For salmon goujons with a minty dip, cut 500 g (1 lb) raw salmon fillets into strips. Mix 2 tablespoons chopped parsley with 100 g (3¹/₂ oz) breadcrumbs and coat each piece of salmon in the mixture. Cook the fish in butter and oil as above for 2–3 minutes until it is cooked and the breadcrumbs are golden, taking care not to break the fish when turning. Mix 300 ml (¹/₂ pint) plain yogurt with 4 tablespoons chopped mint leaves and 3 tablespoons finely diced cucumber. Serve the salmon with the dip in a separate bowl.

caesar salad

Serves **4**
Preparation time **20 minutes**
Cooking time **5 minutes**

1 **garlic clove**, peeled and
    crushed
4 **anchovy fillets** in oil,
    drained and chopped
juice of **1 lemon**
1–2 teaspoons **mustard**
1 **egg yolk**
200 ml (7 fl oz) **olive oil**
vegetable oil, for frying
3 slices of **white bread**, cut
    into cubes
1 **Cos lettuce**, washed and
    torn into pieces
3 tablespoons freshly grated
    Parmesan cheese
pepper

Put the garlic, anchovies, lemon juice, mustard and egg
yolk in a small bowl and sprinkle with pepper. Mix well
until combined. Slowly drizzle in the olive oil, mixing all
the time to make a thick creamy sauce. If the sauce is
too thick, add a little water.

Heat the vegetable oil in a frying pan. Test with one of
the bread cubes to see if it is hot enough; if the bread
sizzles, add the rest of the cubes, turning them when
they are golden brown, then drain on kitchen paper.

Put the lettuce into a large bowl, pour over the
dressing and sprinkle with 2 tablespoons of the
Parmesan; mix well. Sprinkle on the croûtons and
the rest of the Parmesan and serve.

For bacon salad with walnuts & brown croûtons,
make a dressing by mixing 4 tablespoons homemade
mayonnaise with 2 tablespoons white wine vinegar
and 1 teaspoon Dijon mustard. Grill 6 bacon rashers
until crisp and cut into pieces. Toss the bacon with
the torn leaves of 1 Cos lettuce and 50 g (2 oz)
toasted walnut pieces. Make croûtons with wholemeal
bread. Assemble the salad by tossing the ingredients
together and drizzling over the mustard mayonnaise.

hot thai beef salad

Serves **4**
Preparation time **15 minutes**
Cooking time: **5–10 minutes**

2 tablespoons **vegetable oil**
500 g (1 lb) **rump steak** or
  fillet steak, cut into thin
  strips across the grain
3 **garlic cloves**, finely
  chopped
2 **green chillies**, deseeded if
  liked, thinly sliced
8 tablespoons **lemon juice**
1 tablespoon **Thai fish sauce**
2 teaspoons **caster sugar**
2 ripe **papayas**, peeled and
  thinly sliced
½ large **cucumber**, cut into
  matchsticks
75 g (3 oz) **bean sprouts**
1 **crisp lettuce**, shredded
chilli sauce, to serve
  (optional)

Heat the oil in a wok over a moderate heat. Add the steak, garlic and chillies, increase the heat to high and stir-fry for 3–4 minutes, or until the steak is browned on all sides. Pour in the lemon juice and fish sauce, add the sugar and stir-fry until sizzling.

Remove the wok from the heat. Remove the steak from the liquid with a slotted spoon and toss together with the papayas, cucumber, bean sprouts and lettuce.

Drizzle the liquid from the wok over the salad ingredients as a dressing and serve hot with a bowl of chilli sauce, if liked.

For Thai chicken salad with mango & cashews, cut 500 g (1 lb) boneless, skinless chicken breasts into strips and cook with the garlic and chillies as above. Add 8 tablespoons lemon juice, 1 tablespoon fish sauce and 2 teaspoons caster sugar. Chop 2 ripe mangoes. Toss the meat with the mangoes, cucumber matchsticks and bean sprouts. Serve hot on a bed of fresh coriander leaves instead of lettuce, drizzled with the liquid from the wok and sprinkled with 75 g (3 oz) toasted and roughly chopped cashew nuts.

mushrooms on toast

Serves **4**
Preparation time **5 minutes**
Cooking time **20 minutes**

8 large **flat mushrooms**
2 **garlic cloves**, crushed
125 ml (4 fl oz) **extra virgin olive oil**
2 teaspoons chopped **thyme**
finely grated rind and juice of **1 lemon**
2 tablespoons chopped **parsley**
4 slices of **buttered toast**
salt and **pepper**

To serve
rocket
Parmesan cheese shavings

Place the mushrooms, stalk sides up, in a large roasting tin and season with salt and pepper. Put the garlic, oil and thyme in a bowl. Add the lemon rind, reserving some for a garnish, then mix together. Spoon half of the sauce over the mushrooms.

Roast the mushrooms in a preheated oven, 220°C (425°F), Gas Mark 7, for 20 minutes, until tender. Sprinkle with the parsley and drizzle over the lemon juice.

Arrange the mushrooms on the buttered toast, drizzle over the remaining oil mixture and serve topped with some rocket, the remaining lemon rind and some Parmesan.

For oven-roasted garlic tomatoes on ciabatta,
halve 12 large, ripe plum tomatoes lengthways. Roast them in a preheated oven, 220°C (425°F), Gas Mark 7, for 20 minutes with 2 crushed garlic cloves, 125 ml (4 fl oz) olive oil and 2 tablespoons chopped thyme, but omit the lemon juice and rind. Cut a ciabatta loaf in half lengthways and then widthways and rub with a cut garlic clove. Drizzle with 2 tablespoons olive oil, then bake with the tomatoes for the final 10 minutes of cooking. Serve the roasted tomatoes on top of the bread, with Parmesan shavings sprinkled over and drizzled with a little balsamic vinegar.

baked tortillas with hummus

Serves **4**
Preparation time **5 minutes**
Cooking time **10–12 minutes**

4 small wheat **tortillas**
1 tablespoon **olive oil**

Hummus
410 g (13½ oz) can
  chickpeas, drained and
  rinsed
1 **garlic clove**, chopped
4–6 tablespoons **natural
  yogurt**
2 tablespoons **lemon juice**
1 tablespoon fresh **coriander
  leaves**, chopped
salt and **pepper**
paprika, to sprinkle

To serve
lemon wedges
olives

Cut each tortilla into 8 triangles, put on a baking sheet and brush with a little oil. Cook in a preheated oven, 200°C (400°F), Gas Mark 6, for 10–12 minutes, until golden and crisp. Remove from the oven.

Meanwhile, put the chickpeas, garlic, yogurt and lemon juice in a bowl and mix really well until smooth and mushy. Sprinkle with salt and pepper, stir in the coriander and sprinkle with paprika. Serve with the warm tortillas, lemon wedges and olives.

For spicy tortillas with sun-dried tomato & chilli hummus, prepare 4 tortillas as above and brush them with oil. Before baking sprinkle over a little Cajun seasoning. Make a smooth hummus by mixing together 410 g (13^1/$_2$ oz) can chickpeas, 1 garlic clove, 4–6 tablespoons yogurt, 2 tablespoons lemon juice and fresh coriander leaves in a food processor with 3 sun-dried tomatoes, 1 teaspoon chopped red chilli and 2 tablespoons tahini paste. Blend well to form a smooth paste, adding 2–3 tablespoons water if necessary. Season to taste with salt and pepper and serve in a bowl with the warm tortillas.

chips

Serves 4–6
Preparation time **15 minutes**, plus soaking
Cooking time **30 minutes**

900 g (2 lb) **floury potatoes**, such as Estima or Pentland Dell, or all-rounders such as King Edward, Maris Piper or Desirée
vegetable oil, for deep-frying
salt, to sprinkle

Peel the potatoes and cut them into 1.5 cm (¾ inch) slices, then again into batons for chunky chips. For French fries, cut them into slender batons, not much thicker than matchsticks.

Soak the chips in cold water for about 30 minutes to remove any excess starch and stop them sticking together. Drain thoroughly and pat dry between layers of kitchen paper – they must be totally dry before frying, otherwise the oil will splatter.

Put some of the chips into the deep-fat fryer basket and lower them into the preheated fryer, 160˚C (320˚F). (Don't cook too many at a time or they will turn soggy.) Cook for 5 minutes or until they start to soften but not brown. Raise the basket and let the chips drain for 5 minutes. Increase the temperature to 190˚C (375˚F) and lower the chips back into the pan. Fry for about 6–8 minutes, depending on the thickness of the chips, until golden brown.

Drain thoroughly on kitchen paper and sprinkle with salt.

spinach, avocado & bacon salad

Serves **4**

Preparation time **15 minutes**

Cooking time **10 minutes**

1 ripe **avocado**, halved,
  peeled and pitted

2 tablespoons **lemon juice**

500 g (1 lb) **baby spinach
  leaves**

1 small bunch of **spring
  onions**, shredded into long,
  thin strips

2 tablespoons **vegetable oil**

4 rindless **back bacon**
  rashers, chopped

1 **garlic clove**, crushed

Dressing

3 tablespoons **balsamic
  vinegar**

1 teaspoon **light soft
  brown sugar**

1 teaspoon **Dijon mustard**

125 ml (4 fl oz) **olive oil**

1 tablespoon finely chopped
  walnuts, plus extra to
  garnish (optional)

1 tablespoon chopped
  parsley or **basil**

salt and **pepper**

Make the dressing. Mix the vinegar, sugar and mustard in a bowl. Add a dash of salt and pepper, then slowly whisk in the olive oil. Stir the chopped walnuts and herbs into the dressing and add more salt and pepper if needed.

Chop the avocado into cubes and sprinkle with lemon juice to stop it going brown.

Put the spinach leaves in a bowl together with the spring onion strips and avocado cubes.

Heat the oil in a frying pan and fry the bacon and the garlic until crisp and brown, then drain on kitchen paper. Scatter over the spinach mixture.

Drizzle some of the dressing over the salad, toss gently and serve straight away, garnished with extra walnut pieces, if liked.

For warm spinach & stilton salad with walnut croûtons, prepare the salad as above, but omit the bacon. Make the dressing as above and toss the salad in it to coat. Cut off the crusts from 4 slices of brown bread. Butter each slice and sprinkle over 1 tablespoon finely chopped walnuts, then tightly roll and secure with 2 cocktail sticks. Cut each roll in half, keeping a cocktail stick in each half to secure. Heat the oil in a pan and cook the crouton rolls for 1–2 minutes until golden. Remove from the pan and take out the cocktail sticks. Crumble 175 g (6 oz) Stilton cheese into the warm pan, removed from the heat, and allow the cheese to melt slightly. Toss the cheese into the salad and serve each portion with 2 rolls of walnut bread.

drop scones

Makes **8–10**
Preparation time **10 minutes,
 plus standing**
Cooking time **20 minutes**

125 g (4 oz) **self-raising flour**
1 large **egg**
150 ml (¼ pint) **milk**
handful of **dried herbs**
vegetable oil, for frying

Put the flour in a bowl and make a well in the centre. Break the egg into the well and add a little of the milk. Using a balloon whisk, start whisking the egg with the milk. As you do so, the flour will gradually be incorporated into the liquid, thickening it slightly.

Work in more of the flour gradually, whisking continually. As the batter thickens, gradually pour in more milk. Once all the ingredients are combined, add the chopped herbs and pour into a jug. Allow the batter to stand for about 30 minutes before use to give the starch time to swell and produce a less floury result.

Heat a large frying pan or flat griddle and drizzle with a little vegetable oil. Using a spoon or ladle (depending on the size you want to make), drop a little of the batter into the pan, then add more spoonfuls, spacing them slightly apart so that they don't run into each other. Cook for about 1 minute until golden on the underside, then flip the scones with a palette knife to cook the other side. Transfer to a plate and keep warm while you cook the remainder, re-oiling the pan if it becomes too dry.

For wholemeal blueberry scones, combine 125 g (4 oz) wholemeal flour (instead of self-raising flour) with 1 egg and 150 ml (¹/₄ pint milk). Omit the dried herbs and instead add 75 g (3 oz) blueberries. Stir well to mix and cook as above. Serve the warm scones with spoonfuls of natural yogurt and drizzled with maple syrup.

cauliflower cheese

Serves **4**
Preparation time **10 minutes**
Cooking time **15 minutes**

1 large **cauliflower**, divided
  into florets
25 g (1 oz) **butter**
25 g (1 oz) **plain flour**
300 ml (½ pint) **milk**
125 g (4 oz) **Cheddar
  cheese**, grated
1 teaspoon **Dijon mustard**
1 tablespoon **fresh
  breadcrumbs**
salt and **pepper**
4 grilled **back bacon rashers**,
  cut into strips, to garnish

Steam the cauliflower over a pan of lightly salted, boiling water for about 12 minutes until tender. Drain and put in an ovenproof dish.

Meanwhile, melt the butter in a heavy-based saucepan, stir in the flour and cook for 1 minute. Slowly stir in the milk, then two-thirds of the Cheddar and heat, stirring constantly, until the sauce has thickened. Season with mustard, salt and pepper.

Pour the sauce over the cauliflower, sprinkle with the remaining cheese and scatter the breadcrumbs over the top. Put under a medium grill until the top is golden brown. Garnish with bacon strips.

For cauliflower cheese with bacon & seed topping, prepare and cook the cauliflower as above. Make the sauce with 300 ml (½ pint) soya milk and vegetarian cheese and adding 1 tablespoon English mustard. Grill 2 streaky bacon rashers until crisp. Chop the bacon finely and combine with 50 g (2 oz) wholemeal breadcrumbs, 1 tablespoon pumpkin seeds and 1 tablespoon sunflower seeds. Pour the sauce over the cauliflower and scatter over the bacon and seed topping.

herbed soda breads

Makes a **750 g (1½ lb) loaf**
Preparation time **10 minutes**
Cooking time **25–30 minutes**

250 g (8 oz) **wholemeal
  flour**, plus extra for dusting
250 g (8 oz) **plain flour**
1 teaspoon **bicarbonate
  of soda**
1 teaspoon **salt**
50 g (2 oz) **butter**, chilled and
  diced, plus extra for greasing
1 **spring onion**, finely
  chopped
1 tablespoon **chopped
  parsley**
1 tablespoon **chopped thyme**
1 tablespoon **chopped
  rosemary**
275 ml (9 fl oz) **buttermilk**, or
  ordinary **milk** soured with
  1 tablespoon lemon juice

Sift the flours, bicarbonate of soda and salt into a bowl. Add the butter and rub in with your fingertips until the mixture resembles fine breadcrumbs. Add the spring onion and the herbs and mix well to combine. Make a well in the centre and add the buttermilk or soured milk. Mix with a round-bladed knife to make a soft dough. Turn out on to a lightly floured work surface and knead lightly into a ball. Divide the dough between 8 greased dariole moulds.

Place the dariole moulds on a baking sheet, flatten the dough slightly and dust with flour.

Bake in a preheated oven, 220°C (425°F), Gas Mark 7, for about 25–30 minutes until risen, golden and hollow sounding when tapped underneath. Transfer to a wire rack to cool. For a softer crust, wrap the hot bread in a clean tea towel to cool. Eat on the day it is made.

For date & walnut soda breads, omit the spring onion and chopped herbs and add 100 g (3½ oz) light muscovado sugar, 75 g (3 oz) chopped walnuts and 125 g (4 oz) chopped stoned dates. Bake the breads as above.

green bean sambal

Serves **4**
Preparation time **15 minutes**
Cooking time **15 minutes**

2 tablespoons **vegetable oil**
4 **shallots**, thinly sliced
2 **garlic cloves**, crushed
½ teaspoon **shrimp paste**
250 g (8 oz) **French beans**,
   trimmed and thinly sliced
   diagonally
2 teaspoons **sambal oelek**
1 teaspoon **soft brown sugar**
salt

Heat the oil in a wok, add the shallots, garlic and shrimp paste and fry over a low heat, stirring frequently, for 5 minutes, until the shallots are softened.

Add the beans, increase the heat to moderate and fry, stirring occasionally, for 8 minutes, until the beans are cooked but not too soft.

Stir in the sambal oelek, sugar and a little salt and continue frying the beans for a further 1 minute. Taste and add a little more salt if necessary. Serve the sambal hot.

For okra & chilli sambal with raita, cook the shallots, garlic and shrimp paste as above. Instead of the beans, add 250 g (8 oz) okra, each diagonally sliced into 3 pieces. Add 1 small, finely sliced bird's eye chilli with the okra and cook as above. Make a raita by mixing 4 tablespoons natural yogurt with 2 tablespoons chopped fresh coriander, 1 tablespoon chopped mint and 3 tablespoons finely chopped cucumber. Serve the sambal hot with the raita in a bowl.

pasta, rice & noodles

tuna & pasta bake

Serves **4**
Preparation time **5 minutes**
Cooking time **15 minutes**

300 g (10 oz) **pasta shells**
2 tablespoons **olive oil**
1 **onion**, finely chopped
2 **red peppers**, cored,
  deseeded and cubed
2 **garlic cloves**, crushed
200 g (7 oz) **cherry
  tomatoes**, halved
15 g (½ oz) **butter**
50 g (2 oz) **fresh
  breadcrumbs**
400 g (13 oz) can **tuna**,
  drained and flaked
125 g (4 oz) **mozzarella
  cheese** or **Gruyère
  cheese**, grated

Cook the pasta shells in a saucepan of lightly salted boiling water for 8–10 minutes, or according to the packet instructions, until al dente.

Meanwhile, heat the oil in a large frying pan. Add the onion and fry gently for 3 minutes. Add the peppers and garlic and carry on frying, stirring frequently, for 5 minutes. Stir in the tomatoes and fry for 1 minute until they are soft.

Melt the butter in another pan, toss in the breadcrumbs and stir until all the bread is covered in butter.

Drain the pasta, add the pepper and tomato mix, and then the tuna. Mix together, then put in an ovenproof dish.

Sprinkle the mozzarella or Gruyère and then the buttered breadcrumbs over the pasta and cook under a medium grill for 3–5 minutes until the cheese has melted and the breadcrumbs are golden.

For salmon & green bean pasta, cook 300 g (10 oz) pasta as above. Cook the onion and garlic in hot oil. Cut 125 g (4 oz) asparagus into 2.5 cm (1 inch) lengths and trim and halve 125 g (4 oz) fine beans. Add to the pan with the onion and garlic instead of the peppers and cook for 3 minutes. Add the cherry tomatoes as above. Drain and flake 200 g (7 oz) can red salmon and mix with 200 ml (7 fl oz) crème fraîche. Toss all the ingredients together and transfer to an ovenproof dish. Scatter over 50 g (2 oz) breadcrumbs and 125 g (4 oz) grated cheese and cook as above.

quick pasta carbonara

Serves **4**

Preparation time **10 minutes**

Cooking time **10 minutes**

400 g (13 oz) **spaghetti** or other **long thin pasta**

2 tablespoons **olive oil**

1 **onion**, finely chopped

200 g (7 oz) rindless **bacon** or **pancetta**, cut into cubes

2 **garlic cloves**, finely chopped

3 **eggs**

4 tablespoons freshly grated **Parmesan cheese**, plus extra for garnishing

3 tablespoons chopped **parsley**, plus extra for garnishing

3 tablespoons **cream**

salt and **pepper**

Cook the spaghetti in a saucepan of lightly salted boiling water for 8–10 minutes, or according to the packet instructions, until al dente.

Meanwhile, heat the oil in a large frying pan. Add the onion and fry until soft, then add the bacon or pancetta and garlic, and fry gently for 4–5 minutes.

Beat the eggs with the Parmesan, parsley and cream. Season with salt and pepper and mix well.

Drain the spaghetti and add it to the pan with the onion and bacon or pancetta. Stir over a gentle heat until well mixed, then pour in the egg mixture. Stir and take the pan off the heat. Carry on mixing well for a few seconds, until the eggs are lightly cooked and creamy, then serve immediately garnished with Parmesan and parsley.

For quick courgette pasta, use a potato peeler to trim and thinly slice 3 courgettes lengthways into ribbons. Heat the oil in a large, heavy-based frying pan or wok and cook the onions as above, add the courgette ribbons and 2 crushed garlic cloves and cook for 4–5 minutes. Omit the bacon or pancetta. Complete the dish as above and serve with plenty of grated pecorino or Parmesan cheese.

individual macaroni cheeses

Serves **4**
Preparation time **5 minutes**
Cooking time **20 minutes**

250 g (8 oz) **macaroni**
4 **smoked back bacon**
  rashers, diced
1 **garlic clove**, crushed
150 ml (¼ pint) **double cream**
150 ml (¼ pint) **milk**
pinch of freshly grated
  nutmeg
175 g (6 oz) **Cheddar cheese**
  or **Gruyère cheese**, grated
4 tablespoons chopped **basil**
2 **tomatoes**, sliced
salt and **pepper**

Cook the macaroni in a pan of lightly salted boiling water for 8–10 minutes, or according to the packet instructions, until al dente. Drain and place in a bowl.

Meanwhile, dry-fry the bacon in a small frying pan until browned but not crisp. Add the garlic, fry for 1 minute and then add the cream and milk and season with a little nutmeg. Bring just to boiling point.

Stir in 125 g (4 oz) of the Cheddar or Gruyère and all the basil, remove from the heat and stir until the cheese melts. Season to taste with salt and pepper and stir the sauce into the macaroni.

Spoon into individual gratin dishes, top with the sliced tomatoes and remaining cheese and bake in a preheated oven, 230°C (450°F), Gas Mark 8, for 10 minutes, until golden.

For spinach & mixed mushroom macaroni cheese,
cook and drain 250 g (8 oz) macaroni as above. Slice or quarter 300 g (10 oz) mixed mushrooms. Heat 4 tablespoons olive oil in a large, heavy-based frying pan and cook the mushrooms until golden and soft. Add 1 crushed garlic clove and cook for a further minute. Wash and pat dry 400 g (13 oz) fresh spinach and stir through the mushrooms for 1 minute until wilted. Omit the bacon. Stir in the cream and milk as above and flavour with nutmeg and cheese, omitting the basil and tomatoes. Combine the sauce and pasta and cook as above. Serve with plenty of salt and freshly ground black pepper.

seafood spaghetti

Serves **4**

Preparation time **10 minutes**

Cooking time **10 minutes**

300 g (10 oz) **spaghetti**

2 tablespoons **olive oil**

2 **garlic cloves**, crushed

4 **spring onions**, chopped

400 g (13 oz) pack frozen **fruits de mer**, including raw prawns, mussels, scallops and squid, defrosted

200 g (7 oz) raw peeled **king prawns**, defrosted

125 ml (4 fl oz) dry **white wine**

75 ml (3 fl oz) **double cream**

large handful of **flat leaf parsley**, chopped

salt and **pepper**

freshly grated or shaved **Parmesan cheese**, to serve

Cook the spaghetti in a pan of lightly salted boiling water for 8–10 minutes, or according to the packet instructions, until al dente.

Meanwhile, heat the oil in a frying pan, add the garlic and spring onions and cook for 2 minutes. Tip the defrosted shellfish in a sieve, rinse with cold water, drain well, then add to the pan. Fry for 3–4 minutes until the prawns are pink and scallops just cooked.

Lift the shellfish out of the pan with a slotted spoon and reserve. Add the wine and cream to the pan and increase the heat to reduce the sauce.

Return the shellfish to the sauce, stir well and simmer for 2 minutes. Add the parsley and spaghetti, season and mix well, using 2 spoons to combine the spaghetti with the sauce. Serve with Parmesan.

linguine with vegetables

Serves **4**
Preparation time **10 minutes**
Cooking time **10 minutes**

1 **red pepper**, halved, cored
  and deseeded
1 **courgette**, sliced
1 **red onion**, sliced
1 small **aubergine**, sliced into
  thin rounds
8 **asparagus** spears, trimmed
5 tablespoons **olive oil**
300 g (10 oz) **linguine**
3 tablespoons **frozen petits
  pois**
125 g (4 oz) **Parmesan
  cheese**, freshly grated
handful of **basil**, roughly torn
salt and **pepper**

Heat a griddle pan. Add the red pepper, skin side down, and cook until the skin blisters and blackens. Cook the courgette, onion and aubergine slices and the asparagus for 2 minutes on each side. Alternatively, cook all the vegetables under a preheated hot grill.

Peel the skin off the pepper and slice into ribbons. Place in a dish with the courgette, onion, aubergine and asparagus. Drizzle with 4 tablespoons of the oil. Keep warm in a low oven.

Meanwhile, cook the linguine in a pan of lightly salted boiling water for 8–10 minutes, or according to the packet instructions, until al dente. Add the petits pois for the last minute of the cooking time.

Drain the linguine and petits pois, then return to the saucepan. Add the vegetables, seasoning and Parmesan. Toss well, adding the remaining oil if necessary. Add the basil and toss again, then serve.

For linguine in basil-flavoured oil with petits pois,

cook and drain 300 g (10 oz) linguine. Heat 3 tablespoons olive oil in a pan and cook 1 thinly sliced garlic clove for 1 minute. Put 150 ml ($^1/_4$ pint) olive oil in a food processor or blender with a large bunch of basil leaves and the garlic-infused oil. Process to form a green oil. Cook 175 g (6 oz) petits pois and combine with the linguine. Pour the flavoured oil over the pasta and toss well. Serve with grated Parmesan cheese.

spicy mediterranean pasta

Serves **4**
Preparation time **10 minutes**
Cooking time **5 minutes**

125 g (4 oz) pitted **black olives**
1 **red chilli**, deseeded and sliced
4 tablespoons **capers** in brine, drained
2 tablespoons **sun-dried tomato paste**
3 tablespoons chopped **basil**
3 tablespoons chopped **parsley** or **chervil**
4 **tomatoes**, chopped
125 ml (4 fl oz) **olive oil**
375 g (12 oz) fresh **ribbon pasta** or **pasta shapes**
salt and **pepper**
Parmesan cheese shavings, to serve

Place the olives, chilli and capers in a food processor or blender and process until quite finely chopped. Alternatively, finely chop them by hand. Mix with the sun-dried tomato paste, herbs, tomatoes and oil, and season to taste with salt and pepper.

Cook the pasta in plenty of lightly salted boiling water for 2–3 minutes, or according to the packet instructions, until al dente. Drain and return to the saucepan.

Add the olive mixture and toss the ingredients together lightly over a low heat for 2 minutes. Serve sprinkled with Parmesan shavings.

For spicy aubergine pasta with pine nuts, cook and drain 375 g (12 oz) pasta. Roughly chop 1 large aubergine and toss with 4 tablespoons olive oil. Roast in a preheated oven, 200°C (400°F), Gas Mark 6, for 20–25 minutes until turning golden and soft. Toss 125 g (4 oz) olives and a sliced red chilli with 2 tablespoons sun-dried tomato paste, herbs and tomato as above, but omitting the capers and remaining oil. Put in a pan with 4 tablespoons water and the aubergine and heat for 2–3 minutes. Toss with the pasta and serve in warm bowls with lightly toasted pine nuts and Parmesan cheese scattered over and with warm crusty bread on the side.

pepperoni & wilted spinach risotto

Serves **4**
Preparation time **5 minutes**
Cooking time **25 minutes**

50 g (2 oz) **butter**
1 tablespoon **olive oil**
100 g (3½ oz) **pepperoni**,
  thinly sliced
75 g (3 oz) **pine nuts**
1 tablespoon **paprika**
2 **garlic cloves**, crushed
375 g (12 oz) **risotto rice**
1.2 litres (2 pints) hot **chicken
  stock**
250 g (8 oz) **baby spinach
  leaves**
75 g (3 oz) **raisins**
salt and **pepper**

Melt the butter with the oil in a large, heavy-based saucepan. Add the pepperoni and pine nuts and cook gently for about 3 minutes, or until the pine nuts are golden. Drain with a slotted spoon and set aside.

Add the paprika, garlic and rice to the pan and stir well to coat the grains with the butter and oil. Add the hot stock, a large ladleful at a time, stirring until each addition is absorbed into the rice. Continue adding stock in this way, cooking until the rice is creamy but the grains are still firm. This should take about 20 minutes.

Return the pepperoni and pine nuts to the pan with the spinach and raisins. Cook over a gentle heat, stirring the spinach into the rice until wilted. Season to taste with salt and pepper. Cover and leave the risotto to rest for a few minutes before serving.

For chorizo & butternut squash risotto, heat 1 tablespoon olive oil in a pan and cook 175 g (6 oz) thinly sliced chorizo sausage for 2–3 minutes until golden. Cut 350 g (11½ oz) butternut squash into small cubes, add to the pan and cook for a further 2 minutes. Add the rice (omit the garlic) and stir well. Gradually add 1.2 litres (2 pints) stock as above. Serve in warm bowls.

parma ham & sweet potato risotto

Serves **4**
Preparation time **5 minutes**
Cooking time **25 minutes**

2 medium **sweet potatoes**,
   scrubbed and cut into 1 cm
   (½ inch) chunks
50 g (2 oz) **butter**
1 bunch of **spring onions**,
   finely sliced
375 g (12 oz) **risotto rice**
2 **bay leaves**
1.2 litres (2 pints) hot **chicken
   stock** or **vegetable stock**
3 tablespoons **olive oil**
75 g (3 oz) **Parma ham**, torn
   into pieces
25 g (1 oz) **mixed fresh
   herbs,** such as parsley,
   chervil, tarragon and chives,
   chopped
salt and **pepper**

Cook the sweet potatoes in lightly salted boiling water
for 2–3 minutes to soften. Drain and set aside.

Meanwhile, melt the butter in a large, heavy-based
saucepan. Add the spring onions and sauté for
1 minute. Add the rice and stir well to coat the grains
with the butter.

Add the bay leaves to the rice. Add the hot stock, a
large ladleful at a time, stirring until each addition is
absorbed into the rice. Continue adding stock in this
way, cooking until the rice is creamy but the grains are
still firm. This should take about 20 minutes.

Meanwhile, heat 1 tablespoon of the oil in a frying pan
and cook the ham until golden. Drain and keep warm.
Add the remaining oil and fry the sweet potatoes,
turning frequently, for 6–8 minutes, until golden.

Add the herbs to the risotto and season to taste with
salt and pepper, then add the ham and sweet potatoes,
folding in gently. Cover and leave the risotto to rest for
a few minutes before serving.

For roasted tomato, Parma ham & brie risotto,
halve 8 plum tomatoes, season and drizzle over
3 tablespoons olive oil. Roast in a preheated oven,
200°C (400°F), Gas Mark 6, for 30 minutes until
lightly charred and soft. Set aside to cool. Make up
the risotto as above, stirring through the roasted
tomato and 125 g (4 oz) creamy brie cubes at the
end of the cooking instead of the sweet potatoes.
Season generously and serve in warm bowls.

chinese fried rice

Serves **4**

Preparation time **10 minutes,
plus chilling**

Cooking time **10 minutes**

2 tablespoons **vegetable oil**

2 **eggs**, beaten

1 **carrot**, finely diced

75 g (3 oz) frozen **peas**

200 g (7 oz) cooked peeled
prawns, defrosted if frozen

400 g (13 oz) cooked
basmati rice

2 tablespoons **light soy
sauce**

6 **spring onions**, trimmed
and sliced

2 teaspoons **sesame oil**

spring onion curls, to garnish

Heat a wok over a high heat until smoking. Add half
the oil, heat again, then add the eggs and cook until
a thin omelette forms. Loosen and slide out of the pan,
roll up and leave to cool.

Heat the remaining oil, add the carrot and stir-fry for
2 minutes, then add the peas, prawns and rice and
stir-fry for a further 2 minutes.

Add the soy sauce, spring onions and sesame oil and
take off the heat. Mix all together thoroughly and top
with the egg rolls.

Make the spring onion curls for garnishing. Cut
2 onions into 4 cm (1½ inch) lengths, then cut each
piece into very thin strips, add to a bowl of cold water
with two or three ice cubes and leave for 15 minutes
until curled. Drain and serve on top of the fried rice.

For mushroom & egg fried rice, quarter 225 g
(7½ oz) chestnut or oyster mushrooms and cook in
2 tablespoons vegetable oil for 2 minutes or until
golden and soft. Add 400 g (13 oz) rice and stir-fry
as above. Beat 2 eggs with ½ teaspoon five spice
powder, add to the pan and cook as above. Serve
with plenty of soy sauce.

prawns & coconut rice

Serves **4**

Preparation time **10 minutes, plus standing**

Cooking time **15 minutes**

4 tablespoons **groundnut oil**

250 g (8 oz) **Thai fragrant rice**

1 teaspoon **cumin seeds**

1 small **cinnamon stick**

4 **lime leaves**

400 ml (14 fl oz) can **coconut milk**

150 ml (¼ pint) **water**

1 teaspoon **salt**

2 **garlic cloves**, crushed

2.5 cm (1 inch) piece of fresh **root ginger**, peeled and grated

pinch of **crushed dried chillies**

500 g (1 lb) raw **king prawns**, peeled and deveined

2 tablespoons **Thai fish sauce**

1 tablespoon **lime juice**

2 tablespoons chopped fresh **coriander leaves**

25 g (1 oz) **dry-roasted peanuts**, chopped, to garnish

Heat half the oil in a saucepan and stir-fry the rice until all the grains are glossy. Add the cumin seeds, cinnamon stick, lime leaves, coconut milk, measurement water and salt. Bring to the boil and simmer gently over a low heat for 10 minutes. Remove from the heat, cover and leave to rest for 10 minutes.

Meanwhile, heat the remaining oil in a wok and stir-fry the garlic, ginger and crushed dried chillies for 30 seconds. Add the prawns and stir-fry for 3–4 minutes, until pink.

Stir in the coconut rice with the fish sauce, lime juice and coriander. Serve scattered with the peanuts.

For coconut & soya bean rice with lime & cherry tomatoes, cook 250 g (8 oz) rice, adding the cumin seeds, cinnamon stick, lime leaves, coconut milk, water and salt as above. Add 175 g (6 oz) soya beans instead of the prawns. Roughly chop a large handful of fresh coriander leaves and halve 175 g (6 oz) cherry tomatoes. Stir them into the rice together with 1 tablespoon lime juice and the finely grated rind of 1 lime. Stir-fry for 3–4 minutes until hot and cooked through, then serve immediately.

nasi goreng

Serves **4**
Preparation time **10 minutes**
Cooking time **10 minutes**

2 tablespoons **vegetable oil**
150 g (5 oz) boneless,
   skinless **chicken breast**,
   finely chopped
50 g (2 oz) cooked peeled
   prawns, defrosted if frozen
1 **garlic clove**, crushed
1 **carrot**, grated
¼ **white cabbage**, thinly sliced
1 **egg**, beaten
300 g (10 oz) cold cooked
   basmati rice
2 tablespoons **ketchup manis**
   (sweet soy sauce)
½ teaspoon **sesame oil**
1 tablespoon **chilli sauce**
1 **red chilli**, deseeded and cut
   into strips, to garnish

Heat the oil in a wok or large frying pan, add the chicken and stir-fry for 1 minute. Add the prawns, garlic, carrot and cabbage and stir-fry for 3–4 minutes.

Pour in the egg and spread it out using a wooden spoon. Cook until set, then add the rice and break up the egg, stirring it in.

Add the ketchup manis, sesame oil and chilli sauce and heat through. Serve immediately, garnished with the chilli strips.

For vegetarian nasi goring, crush a garlic clove and stir-fry it in 2 tablespoons oil with 1 chopped carrot and ¹/₄ chopped white cabbage. Omit the chicken and prawns but add 1 finely sliced red pepper, 125 g (4 oz) sliced shiitake mushrooms and 2 heads finely shredded pak choi. Stir-fry for a further 2–3 minutes until the vegetables are soft yet still retaining their shape. Add the remaining ingredients and serve in warm serving bowls.

vietnamese beef pho

Serves **4**
Preparation time **5 minutes**
Cooking time **15 minutes**

1.5 litres (2½ pints) **chicken stock**
2 **lemon grass stalks**, bruised
small piece of fresh **root ginger**, sliced
2 tablespoons **light soy sauce**
2 tablespoons **lime juice**
2 teaspoons **soft brown sugar**
125 g (4 oz) **flat rice noodles**
1 tablespoon **sunflower oil**
275 g (9 oz) **sirloin steak**
150 g (5 oz) **bean sprouts**
1 **red chilli**, thinly sliced
handful of **Thai basil leaves**
handful of **mint**

Place the stock, lemon grass, ginger, soy sauce, lime juice and sugar in a large saucepan, bring to the boil and simmer gently for 10 minutes.

Remove the lemon grass and ginger with a slotted spoon and add the noodles. Cook according to the packet instructions.

Meanwhile, heat the oil in a frying pan, add the steak and cook according to taste. Trim off the fat then cut into slices. Ladle the pho into bowls immediately, top with steak slices, bean sprouts, chilli, basil and mint.

For chicken & ginger pho, cook 1.5 litres (2¹/₂ pints) stock as above, doubling the amount of ginger. Replace the steak with 275 g (9 oz) thinly sliced chicken breast. Make carrot flowers by peeling 1 large carrot and trimming the ends. Using a citrus parer, pare the carrot 5 times, spaced apart down its length to form petals, then thinly slice and add them to the pho with 125 g (4 oz) noodles and the chicken. Cook for 4–5 minutes until the chicken is thoroughly cooked. Ladle into warm bowls and top with the bean sprouts, chilli, basil and mint as above.

ginger rice noodles

Serves **4**
Preparation time **10 minutes**
Cooking time **5 minutes**

100 g (3½ oz) **fine rice
noodles**
125 g (4 oz) **green beans**,
halved
finely grated rind and juice
of **2 limes**
1 **Thai chilli**, deseeded and
finely chopped
2.5 cm (1 inch) piece of fresh
root ginger, peeled and
finely chopped
2 teaspoons **caster sugar**
small handful of fresh
coriander leaves, chopped
50 g (2 oz) **dried pineapple
pieces**, chopped

Place the noodles in a bowl, cover with plenty of
boiling water and leave for 4 minutes until soft.

Meanwhile, cook the beans in boiling water for about
3 minutes until tender. Drain.

Mix together the lime rind and juice, chilli, ginger, caster
sugar and coriander in a small bowl.

Drain the noodles and place in a large serving bowl.
Add the cooked beans, pineapple and dressing and
toss together lightly before serving.

For rice noodle & coconut salad, cook the noodles
and beans as above and refresh under cold running
water. Put the noodles and beans in a bowl with
125 g (4 oz) bean sprouts and 125 g (4 oz) shredded
mangetout and toss well. Make the dressing as above
and add 150 ml (¼ pint) coconut milk. Pour the
dressing over the salad and turn to coat. Serve
garnished with fresh coriander leaves.

chicken teriyaki

Serves **4**
Preparation time **5 minutes**,
  plus marinating
Cooking time **5 minutes**

4 boneless, skinless **chicken
  breasts**, about 500 g (1 lb)
  in total, cut into 2.5 cm
  (1 inch) cubes
4 tablespoons **dark soy
  sauce**, plus extra to serve
4 tablespoons **mirin**
2 tablespoons **caster sugar**
250 g (8 oz) **soba noodles**
sesame oil, to serve

Place the chicken in a shallow dish. Combine the soy
sauce, mirin and sugar, add to the chicken and toss well
to coat. Set aside to marinate for 15 minutes.

Meanwhile, cook the noodles according to the packet
instructions, then drain, refresh in iced water, drain
again and chill.

Thread the chicken cubes on to metal skewers and
barbecue or grill for 2–3 minutes on each side.

Toss the noodles with a little sesame oil and serve with
the chicken and extra sesame oil and soy sauce.

For prawn teriyaki with beans & coriander, put
24 large, uncooked prawns in a non-metallic dish.
Make the marinade as above and marinate the prawns
in the mixture for 15 minutes as above. Thinly slice
and blanch 125 g (4 oz) French beans. Toss the
cooked and chilled soba noodles with the sesame oil
and a large handful of fresh coriander leaves. Thread
the prawns on to skewers and cook for 2–3 minutes
on each side. Serve on a bed of green noodles.

chicken with black bean sauce

Serves **4**

Preparation time **10 minutes**

Cooking time **about 20 minutes**

1 **egg white**

1 tablespoon **cornflour**

2 boneless, skinless **chicken breasts**, about 400 g (13 oz) in total, cut into thin strips across the grain

about 300 ml (½ pint) **groundnut oil**

1 **green pepper**, cored, deseeded and cut lengthways into thin strips

1 **green chilli**, deseeded and very finely shredded

4 **garlic cloves**, cut into very thin strips

4 **spring onions**, shredded

4 tablespoons **black bean sauce**

300 ml (½ pint) hot **chicken stock**

salt and **pepper**

1–2 heaped tablespoons canned **fermented black beans**, rinsed, to garnish

egg noodles, to serve

Put the egg white into a bowl with a little salt and pepper and whisk with a fork until frothy. Sift in the cornflour and whisk to mix, then add the chicken and stir until coated.

Heat the oil in a wok until very hot, but not smoking. Add about one-quarter of the chicken strips and stir to separate. Stir-fry for 30–60 seconds, until the chicken turns white on all sides. Lift out with a slotted spoon and drain on kitchen paper. Repeat with the remaining chicken. Very carefully pour off all but about 1 tablespoon of the hot oil from the wok.

Return the wok to a low heat and add the green pepper, chilli, garlic and about half of the spring onions. Stir-fry for a few minutes, until the pepper begins to soften, then add the black bean sauce and stir to mix. Pour in the stock, increase the heat to high and bring to the boil, stirring constantly.

Add the chicken to the sauce and cook over a moderate to high heat, stirring frequently, for 5 minutes. Taste for seasoning. Serve hot with egg noodles, garnished with the remaining spring onions and the black beans.

one pot

sausage & bean casserole

Serves **4**
Preparation time **10 minutes**
Cooking time **20 minutes**

1 tablespoon **oil**
1 **onion**, chopped
1 **garlic clove**, crushed
1 **red pepper**, cored,
    deseeded and chopped
8 lean **pork sausages**, about
    500 g (1 lb) in total,
    quartered
2 x 410 g (13½ oz) cans
    mixed beans, drained and
    rinsed
400 g (13 oz) can **chopped
    tomatoes**
150 ml (¼ pint) **vegetable
    stock**
2 tablespoons **tomato purée**
2 tablespoons chopped
    parsley
salt and **pepper**

Heat the oil in a saucepan, add the onion, garlic and
red pepper and fry for 2–3 minutes until they are
beginning to soften.

Add the sausages and continue to cook for 5 minutes
until browned all over.

Crush half of the beans lightly with the back of a fork
and add to the pan with the remaining beans, the
tomatoes, stock and tomato purée. Season to taste
with salt and pepper. Bring to the boil and simmer for
10 minutes. Remove the pan from the heat, stir in the
parsley and serve.

For rosemary & lamb casserole, cook the onion,
garlic and red pepper as above. Cut 375 g (12 oz)
lean lamb into cubes and add to the saucepan.
Cook for a further 4–5 minutes until golden. Add
3 tablespoons fresh rosemary leaves. Crush 410 g
(13½ oz) flageolet beans and add them to the pan
with the same quantity of whole beans as above. Add
the tomatoes, stock and tomato purée. Season and
bring to the boil and cook for 25–30 minutes until the
lamb is tender. Omit the parsley and serve ladled over
creamy mashed potatoes.

pesto, pea & broccoli soup

Serves **4**
Preparation time **5 minutes**
Cooking time **25 minutes**

2 tablespoons **olive oil**
1 **onion**, finely chopped
1 baking **potato**, about 275 g
  (9 oz), diced
1 **garlic clove**, chopped
200 g (7 oz) can **tomatoes**
900 ml (1½ pints) **vegetable
  stock** or **chicken stock**
175 g (6 oz) **broccoli**, cut into
  tiny florets and stalks sliced
125 g (4 oz) **frozen peas**
2 teaspoons **pesto**, plus extra
  to garnish
salt and **pepper**
a few **basil leaves**, to garnish
freshly grated **Parmesan
  cheese**, to serve

Heat the oil in a large heavy-based saucepan, add the
onion and fry for 5 minutes, until lightly browned. Add
the potato and garlic and fry for 5 further minutes,
stirring, until softened.

Add the tomatoes and stock, and season with salt
and pepper, then bring to the boil. Cover the pan and
simmer for 10 minutes, until reduced and thickened.
Add the broccoli, peas and pesto and simmer for
3–4 minutes, until the broccoli is just tender.

Garnish the soup with a little extra pesto and the basil
and serve with Parmesan.

For pasta & bean soup with pesto, cook the onion
and garlic as above for 3–4 minutes, add the
tomatoes, stock and 125 g (4 oz) fusilli pasta, but
omit the potato, broccoli and peas. Rinse and drain
400 g (13 oz) canned mixed beans and add them to
the pan with 2 teaspoons pesto. Cover and simmer
for 10 minutes until the pasta is tender. Season to
taste with salt and pepper. Ladle into warm serving
bowls, scatter over a few basil leaves and serve
sprinkled with grated Parmesan cheese.

thai chicken curry

Serves **4**

Preparation time **10 minutes**

Cooking time **20 minutes**

1 tablespoon **sunflower oil**

1 **lemon grass stalk**, cut into 4 pieces

2 **kaffir lime leaves**, halved

1–2 **red chillies**, deseeded, if liked, then finely chopped

2.5 cm (1 inch) piece of fresh **root ginger**, peeled and grated

1 **onion**, finely chopped

1 **garlic clove**, crushed

1 **red pepper**, cored, deseeded and chopped

1 **green pepper**, cored, deseeded and chopped

3 boneless, skinless **chicken breasts**, about 500 g (1 lb) in total, chopped

410 g (13½ oz) can **coconut milk**

150 ml (¼ pint) **chicken stock**

2 tablespoons chopped fresh **coriander leaves**

salt and **pepper**

basmati rice, to serve

Heat the oil in a saucepan, add the lemon grass, lime leaves, chilli, ginger, onion and garlic and fry for 2 minutes. Add the red and green peppers and chopped chicken and fry for 5 minutes.

Pour in the coconut milk and the stock and bring to the boil, then reduce the heat and simmer for 10 minutes, or until the chicken is cooked through.

Stir in the coriander leaves and season to taste with salt and pepper. Serve with basmati rice.

For squash & pepper curry, cook the lemon grass, lime leaves, chilli, ginger, onion and garlic as above. Add the peppers to the pan. Omit the chicken and instead add 375 g (12 oz) cubed butternut squash and 2 courgettes, trimmed and cut into chunks. Stir-fry for 5 minutes. Add the coconut milk and stock and cook as above, adding 125 g (4 oz) fine green beans for the final 5 minutes of cooking. Stir in the coriander and serve with sticky Thai rice.

haddock & spinach chowder

Serves **4**
Preparation time **10 minutes**
Cooking time **25 minutes**

50 g (2 oz) **butter**
1 tablespoon **sunflower oil**
1 large **onion**, chopped
1 large baking **potato**, diced
900 ml (1½ pints) semi-
   skimmed **milk**
1 **fish stock cube**
2 **bay leaves**
freshly grated **nutmeg**
400 g (13 oz) **smoked
   haddock fillet**, halved
125 g (4 oz) **baby spinach
   leaves**, stems removed and
   torn into pieces
salt and **pepper**
4 grilled rindless **streaky
   bacon** rashers, to garnish
   (optional)
crusty bread, to serve

Heat the butter and oil in a large heavy-based saucepan, add the onion and fry gently for 5 minutes, until softened but not browned. Add the potato and fry for a further 5 minutes, stirring, until lightly browned.

Stir in the milk, stock cube, bay leaves, nutmeg and salt and pepper to taste. Add the haddock and bring to the boil, then cover the pan and simmer for 10 minutes until the haddock is cooked and flakes easily.

Lift the haddock out of the pan on to a plate, peel off the skin and flake the flesh into pieces, carefully removing any bones, then set aside.

Add the spinach to the pan and cook for 2–3 minutes, until tender. Return the haddock to the pan and reheat.

Garnish the soup with the bacon, if using, and serve with crusty bread.

For prawn & sweetcorn soup, cook the onion and potato as above. Add the milk, stock cube and seasoning but omit the haddock and spinach. Instead add 225 g (7½ oz) prawns and 225 g (7½ oz) sweetcorn. Cook for 2–3 minutes until piping hot, then stir in 6 tablespoons chopped flat leaf parsley. Garnish with bacon as above and serve with warm crusty wholemeal bread.

chicken biryani

Serves **4**

Preparation time **10 minutes**, plus marinating

Cooking time **25 minutes**

250 g (8 oz) boneless, skinless **chicken thighs**, cut into bite-sized pieces

1 teaspoon **turmeric**

1 teaspoon **ground cumin**

1 teaspoon **ground coriander**

1 teaspoon **chilli powder**

6 tablespoons **Greek yogurt**

1 tablespoon **vegetable oil**

1 **onion**, thinly sliced

2 **garlic cloves**, finely chopped

1 teaspoon grated fresh **root ginger**

5 cm (2 inch) piece of **cinnamon stick**

3 **cloves**

3 **cardamom pods**

250 g (8 oz) **basmati rice**

600 ml (1 pint) **chicken stock**

400 g (13 oz) **potatoes**, cut into 2.5 cm (1 inch) chunks

salt and **pepper**

coriander sprigs, to garnish

To serve
poppadums
Indian chutneys

Put the chicken in a bowl with the turmeric, cumin, coriander, chilli and yogurt and mix well. (If you have more time, allow the chicken to marinate for longer. Just cover the bowl with clingfilm, then place in the refrigerator.)

Heat the oil in a heavy-based saucepan. Add the onion, garlic, ginger, cinnamon, cloves and cardamom and fry for 3–4 minutes.

Add the chicken mixture and cook for 2–3 minutes, stirring often. Stir in the rice and pour in the stock. Season generously with salt and pepper and bring to the boil. Add the potatoes, cover the pan tightly and reduce the heat. Simmer gently for 10–12 minutes.

Remove the pan from the heat and leave it to stand, without removing the lid, for 5 minutes. Fluff up the rice with a fork, garnish with sprigs of coriander and serve the biryani with poppadums and Indian chutneys.

mediterranean lamb stew

Serves **4**
Preparation time **15 minutes**
Cooking time **30 minutes**

2 tablespoons **olive oil**
500 g (1 lb) lean **lamb fillet**,
  very thinly sliced
1 **red onion**, chopped
1 large **aubergine**, about
  375 g (12 oz), cut into
  small chunks
2 **garlic cloves**, crushed
400 g (13 oz) can **chopped
  tomatoes**
2 tablespoons **sun-dried
  tomato paste**
1 teaspoon **light muscovado
  sugar**
150 ml (¼ pint) **vegetable
  stock**
salt and **pepper**
crusty bread, to serve

Pesto
½ bunch of **spring onions**,
  trimmed and roughly
  chopped
50 g (2 oz) **Parmesan
  cheese**, crumbled
2 teaspoons **wine vinegar**
  or fresh **lemon juice**
3 tablespoons **olive oil**

Heat 1 tablespoon of the oil in a large flameproof casserole. Add the lamb and fry gently for 5 minutes. Remove the lamb and set aside.

Heat the remaining oil in the casserole, add the onion and aubergine and fry for about 5 minutes until beginning to colour. Add the garlic, tomatoes, tomato paste, sugar and stock and bring to the boil. Reduce the heat, cover the pan and simmer gently for 5 minutes.

Return the lamb to the casserole and stir into the vegetables. Cook gently for 15 minutes. Check the seasoning.

Put the spring onions, Parmesan, wine vinegar or lemon juice and the olive oil into a blender or food processor and whizz to a coarse paste. Transfer this pesto to a small bowl.

Spoon the stew into bowls and top with spoonfuls of pesto. Serve with crusty bread.

For vegetarian Mediterranean stew, trim and cut 2 large courgettes into chunks. Core and deseed 2 red peppers. Cook the onion and aubergine as above, add the courgettes and peppers and cook for 5 minutes. Add the remaining ingredients (omitting the lamb) together with 125 g (4 oz) black olives and cook for 15–20 minutes until all the vegetables are tender. Make a pesto with a large handful of basil leaves instead of the spring onions and add 1 tablespoon pine nuts to the mix while processing. Serve the hot stew with pesto spooned over.

navarin of spring vegetables

Serves **4**
Preparation time **10 minutes**
Cooking time **25 minutes**

250 g (8 oz) small **broad beans**, defrosted if frozen
175 g (6 oz) **sugar snap peas**, trimmed
175 g (6 oz) fine young **asparagus**, trimmed and cut into 2.5 cm (1 inch) pieces
75 g (3 oz) **butter**
8 **spring onions**, sliced
2 **garlic cloves**, chopped
900 ml (1½ pints) **chicken stock** or **vegetable stock**
1 **thyme sprig**
15 **baby onions**, peeled
10 **baby turnips** or 3 small **turnips**, cut into wedges
250 g (8 oz) small **carrots**
1½ tablespoons fresh **lemon juice**
salt and **pepper**
chopped **chervil** or **parsley**, to garnish

Cook the broad beans (if using fresh ones), sugar snap peas and asparagus in salted boiling water for 2–3 minutes, then plunge immediately into a bowl of ice-cold water. This is known as blanching. Drain and set aside. Pop the broad beans out of their skins.

Melt the butter in a large flameproof casserole over a low heat, add the spring onions and garlic and cook, without colouring, for 3 minutes, until softened. Add the stock and thyme and bring to the boil, then add the baby onions. Cover the casserole and simmer for 5 minutes.

Add the turnips, bring back to the boil, then reduce the heat and simmer for 6–8 minutes. Add the carrots and cook for 5–6 minutes. Season with salt, pepper and lemon juice. Add the beans, peas and asparagus and heat through. Serve garnished with the chopped herbs.

For navarin of lamb, blanch the beans, peas and asparagus as above. Heat 75 g (3 oz) butter in a large flameproof casserole dish and lightly fry 4 lamb chops or cutlets for 2 minutes on each side with the garlic (omit the spring onions). Add the stock and thyme and bring to the boil, adding the baby onions, 225 g (7½ oz) scrubbed new potatoes (instead of the turnips) and the carrots. Continue to cook as above, simmering for 5 minutes and then cooking for a further 15 minutes. Add 125 g (4 oz) trimmed baby leeks for the final 5 minutes of cooking. Serve garnished with chopped chervil.

boston baked beans

Serves **4**

Preparation time **10 minutes**

Cooking time **30 minutes**

2 tablespoons **vegetable oil**

1 large **red onion**, finely chopped

4 **celery sticks**, finely chopped

2 **garlic cloves**, crushed

400 g (13 oz) can **chopped tomatoes**

300 ml (½ pint) **vegetable stock**

2 tablespoons **dark soy sauce**

2 tablespoons **dark brown sugar**

4 teaspoons **Dijon mustard**

2 x 410 g (13½ oz) cans **mixed beans**, drained and rinsed

4 tablespoons chopped **parsley**

buttered toast, to serve

Heat the oil in a heavy-based saucepan. Add the onion and cook over a low heat for 5 minutes, or until softened. Add the celery and garlic and continue to cook for 1–2 minutes.

Add the tomatoes, stock and soy sauce and bring to the boil, then reduce the heat to a fast simmer and cook for about 15 minutes, or until the sauce begins to thicken.

Add the sugar, mustard and mixed beans and cook for a further 5 minutes, or until the beans are heated through. Stir in the chopped parsley and serve on toast.

For baked beans with bacon & grilled cheese, cook the onion, celery and garlic as above together with 125 g (4 oz) chunky bacon pieces for 5 minutes. Add the tomatoes. Omit the stock and soy sauce and instead add 6 tablespoons tomato purée and 4 tablespoons water. Cook as above. Add the sugar, mustard and beans and cook as above. Spoon on to slices of toast. Sprinkle 25 g (1 oz) grated Cheddar cheese over each portion and cook under a hot grill for 2–3 minutes until melted and golden. Serve immediately.

chicken & lemon paella

Serves **4**
Preparation time **10 minutes**
Cooking time **30–40 minutes**

2 tablespoons **olive oil**
500 g (1 lb) boneless, skinless
 chicken thighs, diced
2 **onions**, sliced
3 **garlic cloves**, crushed
1 **red pepper**, cored,
 deseeded and roughly
 chopped
200 g (7 oz) **easy-cook long-
 grain rice**
4 tablespoons **dry sherry**
450 ml (¾ pint) **chicken stock**
200 g (7 oz) **frozen peas**
grated rind and juice of
 1 lemon
salt and **pepper**
thyme sprigs, to garnish
lemon wedges, to serve

Heat 1 teaspoon of the oil in a frying pan over a medium heat and cook the chicken for 4–6 minutes, or until golden. Remove from the pan and add the remaining oil. Add the onion and cook over a medium heat for 10 minutes until soft. Add the garlic and red pepper and cook for 3 minutes.

Stir in the rice and pour in the sherry and stock. Return the chicken to the pan. Turn the heat to low and cook for 10–15 minutes.

Add the peas and cook for a further 2–3 minutes, or until the liquid has evaporated. Stir in the lemon rind and juice, then season to taste with salt and pepper. Serve garnished with thyme sprigs and accompanied by lemon wedges.

For chorizo, prawn & chicken paella, cook the chicken as above. With the chicken in the pan, add the onions, garlic and red pepper together with 175 g (6 oz) thinly sliced chorizo sausage. Cook as above. Stir in the rice, sherry and stock, omitting the peas, and cook for 10–15 minutes. Stir in the lemon rind and juice with 125 g (4 oz) prawns and cook for a further 2–3 minutes until the prawns are piping hot. Add 6 tablespoons chopped parsley and season to taste. Serve piping hot.

vegetable curry

Serves **4**
Preparation time **10 minutes**
Cooking time **20–25 minutes**

1 tablespoon **olive oil**
1 **onion**, chopped
1 **garlic clove**, crushed
2 tablespoons **medium
curry paste**
1.5 kg (3 lb) prepared **mixed
vegetables**, such as
courgettes, peppers, squash,
mushrooms and green beans
200 g (7 oz) can **chopped
tomatoes**
410 g (13½ oz) can **coconut
milk**
2 tablespoons chopped fresh
coriander leaves
rice, to serve

Heat the oil in a large saucepan, add the onion and
garlic and fry for 2 minutes. Stir in the curry paste and
fry for 1 minute more.

Add the vegetables and fry for 2–3 minutes, stirring
occasionally, then add the tomatoes and coconut milk.
Stir well and bring to the boil, then lower the heat and
simmer for 12–15 minutes until all the vegetables are
cooked. Stir in the coriander and serve with rice.

For mango & chicken curry, cut 500 g (1 lb) chicken
fillet into cubes. Heat the oil and cook the onion, garlic
and chicken for 5 minutes, adding the curry paste for
the final minute. Remove the stone from 2 mangoes
and cut the flesh into cubes. Add the mango to the
pan and stir-fry for 1 minute. Add the tomatoes and
coconut milk, cover and simmer for 12–15 minutes
until the chicken is cooked. Stir in the fresh coriander
leaves and serve with rice.

meaty treats

rolled stuffed chicken breasts

Serves **4**
Preparation time **10 minutes**
Cooking time **20 minutes**

4 boneless, skinless **chicken
  breasts**, about 150 g (5 oz)
  each
4 slices of **Parma ham**
4 thin slices of **buffalo
  mozzarella cheese**
4 **asparagus** tips, plus extra
  to serve
75 g (3 oz) **plain flour**
1 tablespoon **olive oil**
50 g (2 oz) **butter**
50 ml (2 fl oz) dry **white wine**
75 ml (3 fl oz) **chicken stock**
200 g (7 oz) **baby leaf
  spinach**
200 g (7 oz) chilled pack
  sun-blush tomatoes in oil,
  drained
salt and **pepper**

Place each chicken breast between 2 sheets of
greaseproof paper and flatten to about 2½ times its
original size by pounding with a rolling pin.

Season the chicken with salt and pepper, place a slice
of Parma ham, a slice of mozzarella and an asparagus
tip on top and tightly roll up the chicken breasts. Tie
with a piece of strong thread or spear with wooden
cocktail sticks.

Season the flour with salt and pepper. Dip the
prepared chicken rolls into the flour to coat evenly.

Heat the oil and half of the butter in a frying pan,
add the chicken rolls and sauté over a low heat for
15 minutes or until golden all over and cooked through,
turning frequently to brown the chicken evenly.

Remove the chicken, place in a warmed serving dish
and keep warm. Pour the wine and stock into the pan,
bring to the boil and simmer for 3 minutes.

Remove the thread or cocktail sticks just before serving
the chicken. Add the remaining butter to the pan, mix
quickly with a small whisk to emulsify the sauce, add
the spinach and tomatoes and cook for 2 minutes
until the spinach has just wilted. Spoon on to plates,
slice the chicken and arrange in a line down the centre.

For cheese & tomato stuffed chicken, prepare the
chicken breasts as above. Spread each with 50 g
(2 oz) soft goats' cheese and top with 4 basil leaves
and 3 sun-blushed tomatoes. Roll up tightly and
secure with thread or cocktail sticks as above.
Continue to cook as above. Serve with fine green
beans tossed with a little lemon butter.

kashmiri lamb chops

Serves **4**

Preparation time **10 minutes**, plus marinating

Cooking time **8–12 minutes**

150 ml (¼ pint) **natural yogurt**

1 teaspoon **chilli powder**

2 teaspoons grated fresh **root ginger**

2 **garlic cloves**, crushed

2 tablespoons chopped **fresh coriander**

1 tablespoon **sunflower oil**, plus extra for oiling

8 **lamb loin chops**

salt and **pepper**

To serve

pilau rice

cherry tomato, onion and coriander salad

Mix together the yogurt, chilli powder, ginger, garlic, coriander and oil in a large bowl and season with salt and pepper.

Add the chops to this mixture and coat them thoroughly. Cover and marinate for at least 3 hours (ideally 10 hours) in the refrigerator, if time allows.

Place the chops on a lightly oiled grill pan. Cook under a preheated hot grill for 4–6 minutes on each side or until tender. Serve with pilau rice and a cherry tomato, onion and coriander salad.

For lamb & apricot kebabs, cut 375 g (12 oz) lamb fillet into cubes. Prepare the marinade as above. Coat the lamb thoroughly in the marinade and leave as above. Thread the lamb on to skewers, alternating the meat with red onion wedges and dried apricots. Cook the skewers on the barbecue or griddle or under the grill for 4–6 minutes on each side until cooked through. Serve with brown rice.

spicy beef burgers

Serves **4**
Preparation time **10 minutes**
Cooking time **6–14 minutes**

575 g (1 lb 3 oz) lean **minced beef**
2 **garlic cloves**, crushed
1 **red onion**, finely chopped
1 **hot red chilli**, finely chopped
1 bunch of **parsley**, chopped
1 tablespoon **Worcestershire sauce**
1 **egg**, beaten
4 **rolls**, such as wholemeal or Granary, split
hot salad leaves, such as mizuna or rocket
1 **beefsteak tomato**, sliced
salt and **pepper**
snipped **chives**, to garnish

To serve
burger relish
griddled new potatoes

Put the minced beef, garlic, red onion, chilli and parsley in a large bowl. Add the Worcestershire sauce, beaten egg and a little salt and pepper and mix well.

Heat a griddle pan. Using your hands, divide the minced meat mixture into 4 and shape into burgers. Cook the burgers in the griddle pan for 3 minutes on each side for rare, 5 minutes for medium or 7 minutes for well done.

Place the roll halves under a preheated hot grill and toast on one side. Fill each bun with some hot salad leaves, some tomato slices and a griddled burger, garnish with snipped chives and serve with your favourite relish and griddled new potatoes.

For pork & apple burgers, mix 575 g (1 lb 3 oz) pork mince with the garlic, red onion, chilli and parsley in a large bowl as above. Peel, core and finely chop 1 small red apple and add to the bowl. Omit the Worcestershire sauce, but add the egg to the bowl and season well. Shape the mixture into burgers and cook. Grate Wensleydale cheese over the top while the burgers are warm and serve in the halved rolls as above.

sausages with mustard mash

Serves **4**
Preparation time **5 minutes**
Cooking time **25 minutes**

8 **sausages**
2 **onions**, cut into wedges
2 **dessert apples**, cored and
   cut into wedges
1 tablespoon **plain flour**
200 ml (7 fl oz) **chicken stock**

Mustard mash
1 kg (2 lb) **potatoes**,
   quartered and scrubbed
75 g (3 oz) **butter**
1–2 tablespoons wholegrain
   mustard
1 **garlic clove**, crushed
salt and **pepper**
1 large bunch of **parsley**,
   chopped
dash of **olive oil**

Put the potatoes into a large saucepan of cold water, bring to the boil and simmer for 15 minutes until tender.

Meanwhile, fry or grill the sausages over a medium heat for 10 minutes, turning to get an even colour. Add the onion and apple wedges and cook with the sausages for 6–7 minutes.

Drain the potatoes well. When they are cool enough to touch, peel them, then mash well so they are nice and creamy.

Add the butter, mustard, garlic and a good sprinkling of salt and pepper to the potatoes, and carry on mashing. Taste and add more mustard if you want. Finally, stir in the parsley and olive oil.

Transfer the sausages, onion and apple to a serving plate. Pour off the excess fat from the pan to leave about 1 tablespoon, then mix in the flour. Gradually stir in the stock, bring to the boil and stir until thickened. Season and strain into a jug.

Pile the mash up on a plate and stick the sausages and onion wedges on top. Spoon over the gravy and serve.

For cheesy mash with stir-fried leeks, finely slice 2 medium leeks. Heat 50 g (2 oz) butter in a pan and cook the leeks for 5–6 minutes over a gentle heat until softened and beginning to turn golden in places. Set aside. Cook and mash the potatoes as above, but omit the garlic and instead add 125 g (4 oz) grated Cheddar cheese. Stir well to mix and make a creamy mash. Fold through the stir-fried leeks and season well. Serve with the sausages as above.

chargrilled chicken with salsa

Serves **4**

Preparation time **10 minutes**,
plus marinating

Cooking time **18 minutes**

2 tablespoons **dark soy
sauce**

2 teaspoons **sesame oil**

1 tablespoon **olive oil**

2 teaspoons **clear honey**

pinch of crushed **dried
chillies**

4 large boneless, skinless
chicken breasts, about
200 g (7 oz) each

Salsa

1 **red onion**, diced

1 small **garlic clove**, crushed

1 bunch of fresh **coriander
leaves**, roughly chopped

6 tablespoons **extra virgin
olive oil**

grated rind and juice of
1 lemon

1 teaspoon **ground cumin**

salt and **pepper**

To serve

diced **tomato**

couscous

Combine the soy sauce, sesame oil, olive oil, honey
and crushed dried chillies in a shallow dish. Add the
whole chicken breasts, cover and leave to marinate for
3–4 hours in the refrigerator.

Preheat a griddle pan over a high heat until hot, then
add the chicken, reduce the heat to medium, and cook
for 8 minutes on each side, until char-grilled and
cooked through. Wrap in foil and leave to rest for
5 minutes.

Meanwhile, mix all the salsa ingredients together and
season with salt and pepper. Set aside to infuse.

Strain the marinade juices into a small saucepan and
bring to the boil, then remove from the heat.

Serve the chicken with the couscous tossed with diced
tomato and top with the salsa and the warm marinade.

For salmon with mango & chilli salsa, prepare
the marinade as above. Coat 4 salmon fillets, each
about 175 g (6 oz), in the marinade and leave at
room temperature for 2 hours before griddling for
2–3 minutes on each side until slightly blackened. Cut
1/2 mango into small dice. Prepare the salsa as above,
but with 1/2 red onion and omitting the garlic. Add the
mango. Finely slice a bird's eye chilli and stir through
the salsa. Serve the hot salmon with the salsa
spooned over.

lamb fillet with beetroot salad

Serves **4**
Preparation time **5 minutes**
Cooking time **20 minutes**

125 g (4 oz) **Puy lentils**
125 g (4 oz) fine **green beans**
4 tablespoons **extra virgin olive oil**
2 **best end of neck fillets** or **lamb loins**, about 300 g (10 oz) each
4 tablespoons **red wine**
1 tablespoon **red wine vinegar**
375 g (12 oz) **cooked beetroot** in natural juices, drained and diced
1 small bunch of **mint**, roughly chopped
salt and **pepper**

Put the lentils into a saucepan, cover with cold water and simmer for 20 minutes. Drain well and transfer to a bowl.

Meanwhile, cook the green beans in salted boiling water for 2–3 minutes, then plunge immediately into a bowl of ice-cold water. This is known as blanching. Drain and pat dry on kitchen paper.

Heat 1 tablespoon of the oil in a frying pan and fry the lamb fillets for 7 minutes, turning once. Transfer to a low oven, 150°C (300°F), Gas Mark 2, to rest for 5 minutes, reserving the juices in the pan.

Add the wine to the pan juices and boil until only about 1 tablespoon remains. Remove from the heat and whisk in the vinegar and the remaining oil and season to taste with salt and pepper.

Combine the lentils, beans, beetroot and mint in a bowl, add the dressing and toss to coat. Serve with the lamb.

For bacon & Puy lentil salad, heat 1 tablespoon olive oil in a large, heavy-based frying pan and cook 1 large, finely chopped onion for 3–4 minutes until softened. Add 125 g (4 oz) roughly chopped back bacon and cook for a further 3–4 minutes until golden. Add the lentils as above together with 300 ml (1/2 pint) chicken stock and bring to the boil. Reduce the heat, cover and simmer for 20 minutes until the lentils are cooked, adding more water if necessary. Cook the green beans as above and plunge into cold water. Mix the beans with the warm lentils and serve.

beef steaks with mozzarella

Serves **4**
Preparation time **10 minutes**
Cooking time **18–22 minutes**

2 tablespoons **vegetable oil**
4 rump or sirloin **beef steaks**,
   about 250 g (8 oz) each
2 tablespoons **olive oil**
1 **onion**, finely chopped
1 **garlic clove**, crushed
1 **courgette**, diced
1 **yellow pepper**, cored,
   deseeded and diced
1 **aubergine**, diced
6 **plum tomatoes**, skinned
   and diced
10 **basil leaves**, chopped
4 thick slices of **mozzarella**
   cheese
salt and **pepper**
basil or **flat leaf parsley**
   sprigs, to garnish

Heat the vegetable oil in a shallow pan over a medium heat. Add the steaks and cook for about 2–4 minutes on each side, or according to taste. Season, remove from the pan and keep warm.

Add the olive oil to the same pan and sauté the onion and garlic until golden and crispy. Add the courgette, yellow pepper and aubergine, and cook for a few minutes. Add the tomatoes to the pan with a little salt and pepper, then add the basil.

Place the steaks on a baking sheet. Top each one with a quarter of the vegetables and a thick slice of mozzarella. Place in a preheated oven, 200°C (400°F), Gas Mark 6, for about 5 minutes, or until the mozzarella is slightly melted. Serve garnished with a sprig of basil or parsley.

For cod steaks with Cheddar cheese, sprinkle lemon juice over 4 cod loins, each about 175 g (6 oz), and season to taste with salt and pepper. Prepare the vegetable mixture as above. Arrange the fish on a lightly greased baking sheet and spoon over the vegetable mixture. Top with thick slices of Cheddar cheese. Bake as above for about 15 minutes or until the fish is opaque and cooked through and the cheese has melted.

roast pork with fennel

Serves **4**
Preparation time **10 minutes**
Cooking time **30 minutes**

625 g (1¼ lb) **pork fillet**
1 large **rosemary sprig**,
    broken into short lengths,
    plus extra sprigs to garnish
3 **garlic cloves**, peeled and
    sliced
4 tablespoons **olive oil**
1 large **fennel bulb**, trimmed
    and cut into wedges, central
    core removed
1 large **red onion**, cut into
    wedges
1 large **red pepper**, halved,
    deseeded and cut into
    chunks
150 ml (¼ pint) **white wine**
75 g (3 oz) **mascarpone
    cheese** (optional)
salt and **pepper**

Pierce the pork with a sharp knife and insert the pieces of rosemary and garlic evenly all over the fillet. Heat half the oil in a roasting tin on the hob, add the pork and cook for 5 minutes or until browned all over.

Add the fennel, onion and red pepper to the roasting tin and drizzle the vegetables with the remaining oil. Season well with salt and pepper. Roast in a preheated oven, 230°C (450°F), Gas Mark 8, for 20 minutes or until the juices run clear when the pork is pierced in the centre with a knife.

Transfer the pork and vegetables to a serving plate and keep hot in the oven. Add the wine to the roasting tin and simmer on the hob until slightly reduced. Stir in the mascarpone, if using.

Cut the pork into slices and arrange on serving plates with spoonfuls of the roasted vegetables and a spoonful or two of the sauce. Serve immediately garnished with rosemary sprigs.

For roast pork with apples & cider sauce, pierce the pork, flavour with rosemary and fry as above. Thickly slice 6 apples with assorted colour skins. Heat 50 g (2 oz) butter and 1 tablespoon olive oil in a large frying pan and fry the onion, red pepper and apples for 4–5 minutes over a moderately high heat until golden and soft. Transfer to a roasting tin, arrange the pork on top and roast as above. Keep the meat and vegetables warm. Make the sauce as above with 150 ml (¹/₄ pint) cider instead of wine and reduce before stirring in the mascarpone and 1 teaspoon Dijon mustard. Season to taste and serve as above.

cashew nut chicken

Serves **4**
Preparation time **10 minutes**
Cooking time **20 minutes**

1 **onion**, roughly chopped
4 tablespoons **tomato purée**
50 g (2 oz) **cashew nuts**
2 teaspoons **garam masala**
2 **garlic cloves**, crushed
1 tablespoon **lemon juice**
¼ teaspoon **turmeric**
2 teaspoons **sea salt**
1 tablespoon **natural yogurt**
2 tablespoons **vegetable oil**
3 tablespoons chopped fresh
   coriander leaves, plus extra
   to garnish
50 g (2 oz) ready-to-eat **dried
   apricots**, chopped
500 g (1 lb) **chicken thighs**,
   skinned, boned and cut into
   bite-sized pieces
300 ml (½ pint) **chicken stock**
toasted **cashew nuts**,
   to garnish

To serve
rice
poppadums

Put the onion, tomato purée, cashew nuts, garam masala, garlic, lemon juice, turmeric, salt and yogurt into a food processor or blender and process until fairly smooth. Set aside.

Heat the oil in a large, nonstick frying pan and, when hot, pour in the spice mixture. Fry, stirring, for 2 minutes over a medium heat. Add half the coriander, the apricots and chicken to the pan and stir-fry for 1 minute.

Pour in the stock, cover and simmer for 10–12 minutes or until the chicken is cooked through and tender. Stir in the remaining coriander and serve with rice and poppadums, garnished with toasted cashew nuts and extra coriander.

For prawns with cashews & mangetout, make the spice mixture as above and fry over a low heat for 2 minutes. Omit the chicken and apricots, but add half the fresh coriander as above together with 300 g (10 oz) prawns and 175 g (6 oz) halved mangetout. Stir-fry for 1–2 minutes, then add the stock. Cover and cook as above. Garnish with the remaining coriander and the cashew nuts and serve immediately.

kheema aloo

Serves **4**
Preparation time **10 minutes**
Cooking time **15–20 minutes**

1 tablespoon **vegetable oil**
4 **cardamom pods**
1 **cinnamon stick**
3 **cloves**
2 **onions**, finely chopped
375 g (12 oz) **minced lamb**
2 teaspoons **garam masala**
2 teaspoons **chilli powder**
2 **garlic cloves**, crushed
2 teaspoons grated fresh **root ginger**
2 teaspoons **salt**
200 g (7 oz) **potatoes**, cut into 1 cm (½ inch) cubes
200 g (7 oz) can **chopped tomatoes**
100 ml (3½ fl oz) hot **water**
4 tablespoons chopped fresh **coriander leaves**
rice or **flatbread**, to serve

Heat the oil in a nonstick frying pan and, when hot, add the cardamom, cinnamon and cloves. Fry for 1 minute, then add the onions and fry, stirring, for 3–4 minutes.

Add the lamb to the pan with the garam masala, chilli powder, garlic, ginger and salt. Stir well to break up the mince and fry for 5–7 minutes.

Add the potatoes, tomatoes and the measurement hot water, cover and simmer gently for 5 minutes or until the potatoes are tender.

Stir in the coriander and serve with rice or flatbread.

For aubergine curry, finely chop 1 large aubergine. Cook the spices and onion as above. Omit the mince. Add 3 more tablespoons vegetable oil to the pan, add the aubergine and cook for a further 5–7 minutes. Add the spices, potatoes, tomatoes and water and simmer gently as above. Add 400 g (13 oz) fresh washed spinach leaves to the pan for the final 3 minutes of cooking. Stir in the coriander and serve with rice or warm naan bread.

beef stroganoff

Serves **4**
Preparation time **10 minutes**
Cooking time **15 minutes**

50 g (2 oz) **butter**
3 **onions**, finely chopped
250 g (8 oz) **button
mushrooms**, thinly sliced
1 **green pepper**, deseeded
and cut into fine strips
500 g (1 lb) **fillet steak** or
good **rump steak**, cut into
strips 5 cm (2 in) long and
5 mm (¼ inch) thick
150 ml (¼ pint) **soured cream**
salt and **pepper**
1 teaspoon chopped **parsley**,
to garnish

Melt half the butter in a large deep frying pan and fry the onions until pale golden. Add the mushrooms and green pepper to the pan and cook for 5 minutes. Remove the onions, mushrooms and green pepper from the pan.

Melt the remaining butter and heat, then fry the steak strips for about 4 minutes, turning so they are cooked evenly.

Return the onions, mushrooms and peppers to the pan and season well, then stir in the soured cream and blend well. Heat until piping hot, but do not allow to boil. Garnish with chopped parsley.

For mixed mushroom stroganoff, cook the onions in the butter as above. Halve or quarter 750 g (1½ lb) assorted mushrooms, such as chestnut, common, oyster, shiitake or wild, or leave them whole if small, and add to the pan. Omit the green pepper and cook the mushrooms over a high heat for 4 minutes. Add 1 tablespoon brandy to the pan and stir to mix. Add 300 ml (½ pint) soured cream mixed with 1 tablespoon wholegrain mustard to the pan and heat for 1 minute, stirring continually, until piping hot. Garnish with parsley and serve with rice.

sweet & sour pork

Serves **4**

Preparation time **10 minutes**

Cooking time **10 minutes**

2 tablespoons **vegetable oil**

300 g (10 oz) **pork fillet**,
thinly sliced

1 large **onion**, sliced

2 **tomatoes**, quartered

½ **cucumber**, cut into chunks

125 g (4 oz) tinned **pineapple
chunks**, drained

1 **green pepper** or **red
pepper**, cored, deseeded
and thinly sliced

300 ml (½ pint) ready-made
sweet and sour sauce

rice or **noodles**, to serve

Heat the oil in a wok or large frying pan until really hot.
Add the pork and onion and stir-fry over a high heat for
about 2–3 minutes until just beginning to brown.

Add the tomatoes, cucumber, pineapple and pepper
and stir-fry for another 3 minutes.

Add the sweet and sour sauce and mix well, stirring
constantly for 1 minute. Serve with rice or noodles.

For sweet & sour pork balls, mix 250 g (8 oz) finely
minced pork in a bowl with 1 teaspoon five spice
powder and 2 teaspoons finely grated fresh ginger
and mix well. Shape into 16 walnut-sized balls and
chill for 10 minutes. Make up a batter with 75 g (3 oz)
plain flour, 4 tablespoons cornflour, 2 teaspoons
baking powder and a pinch of salt. Whisk with 175 ml
(6 fl oz) water and 1 tablespoon sesame oil until a
smooth batter is formed. Half-fill a medium-sized pan
with vegetable oil and heat until a cube of bread turns
golden in 30 seconds. Dip each of the pork balls into
the batter, quickly drop them into the hot oil and cook
for 2–3 minutes until golden and crisp. Remove from
the oil with a slotted spoon and drain on kitchen
paper. Stir-fry the other ingredients as above (except
the pork fillet), adding the fried pork balls at the end.

chicken with chilli jam

Serves **4**
Preparation time **5 minutes**
Cooking time **25 minutes**

4 boneless, skinless **chicken breasts**, about 125 g (4 oz) each
fresh **coriander leaves**, to garnish
rice noodles, to serve

Chilli jam
125 g (4 oz) mild **red chillies**, cored, deseeded and chopped
1 **garlic clove**, crushed
1 **onion**, chopped
5 cm (2 inch) piece of fresh **root ginger**, peeled and chopped
125 ml (4 fl oz) **white vinegar**
500 g (1 lb) **sugar**

Place all the chilli jam ingredients in a small saucepan and bring to the boil, then reduce the heat and simmer for 15 minutes. The mixture should be thick, sticky and jam-like, and will become more so as it cools.

Meanwhile, heat a griddle pan. Place the chicken breasts in the pan, skin side down, and cook for 10 minutes. Turn the chicken over and cook for a further 10 minutes.

Serve the chicken on a bed of noodles, with some of the chilli jam poured over the top, and garnish with coriander. Store any remaining chilli jam in the refrigerator, covered, for up to 1 week, and use it as an accompaniment to spice up other griddled meats.

For chilli jam & warm chicken sandwich, lightly toast 4 slices of wholemeal or granary bread. Spread a generous spoonful of chilli jam over 2 slices and 1 tablespoon mayonnaise over the other slices. Griddle the chicken breast as above and cut into thin slices. Pile the chicken slices on the chilli jam and add plenty of fresh coriander leaves. Top with the mayonnaise-covered slices, sandwich together and cut into triangles. Serve warm.

tangerine beef

Serves **4**
Preparation time **about 15 minutes**, plus freezing, soaking and marinating
Cooking time **15 minutes**

1 piece of **rump steak**, weighing about 500 g (1 lb)
3 tablespoons **groundnut oil**
4 **shallots**, cut lengthways into chunks
200 ml (7 fl oz) **beef stock**
2 tablespoons **soy sauce**
2 tablespoons **Chinese rice wine** or **dry sherry**
3 **tangerines**, peeled and segmented
1 **green chilli**, deseeded and very finely chopped
1–2 teaspoons **sugar**
salt and **pepper**
½ bunch of **fresh coriander**, roughly chopped, to garnish

Marinade
2 pieces of **dried citrus peel** or grated rind of **1 orange**
2 tablespoons **soy sauce**
1 tablespoon **rice wine vinegar**
1 tablespoon **cornflour**
1 teaspoon **sugar**

Wrap the beef in clingfilm and place in the freezer for 1–2 hours until it has become quite firm. Meanwhile, if using, soak the pieces of citrus peel for the marinade in hot water for about 30 minutes until softened, then drain and chop finely.

Remove the beef from the freezer, unwrap it and slice it into thin strips against the grain. Put the strips in a non-metallic dish. Whisk together all the marinade ingredients, including the grated orange rind, if using, pour over the beef and stir to coat thoroughly. Set aside to marinate at room temperature for about 30 minutes, or until the beef is completely thawed.

Preheat a wok or large, heavy-based frying pan. Add 1 tablespoon of the oil, swirl it around the pan and heat until hot. Add about half the beef and stir-fry over a high heat for 3 minutes. Transfer the beef to a plate using a slotted spoon. Add 1 further tablespoon of oil to the pan and stir-fry the remaining beef in the same way. Transfer to the plate using a slotted spoon.

Heat the remaining oil in the wok or pan, then add the shallots, stock, soy sauce, rice wine or sherry and any juice from the tangerines. Sprinkle in the chilli, sugar to taste and a little salt and pepper. Bring to the boil, stirring constantly, then cook for about 5 minutes, until the liquid has reduced.

Return the beef to the pan and toss for 1–2 minutes until all the ingredients are coated with the sauce. Add about two-thirds of the tangerine segments and toss quickly to mix, then taste for seasoning. Serve hot, garnished with the remaining tangerine and coriander.

chorizo & chickpea stew

Serves **4**
Preparation time **5 minutes**
Cooking time **25 minutes**

500 g (1 lb) **new potatoes**
1 teaspoon **olive oil**
2 **red onions**, chopped
2 **red peppers**, cored,
  deseeded and chopped
100 g (3½ oz) **chorizo
  sausage**, thinly sliced
500 g (1 lb) **plum tomatoes**,
  chopped, or 400 g (13 oz)
  can **chopped tomatoes**,
  drained
410 g (13½ oz) can
  chickpeas, drained and
  rinsed
2 tablespoons chopped
  parsley, to garnish
garlic bread, to serve

Bring a saucepan of water to the boil. Add the potatoes and cook for 12–15 minutes until tender. Drain, then slice.

Meanwhile, heat the oil in a large frying pan, add the onions and red peppers and cook for 3–4 minutes. Add the chorizo and cook for 2 minutes.

Add the potato slices, tomatoes and chickpeas and bring to the boil. Reduce the heat and simmer for 10 minutes. Scatter over the parsley and serve with some hot garlic bread to mop up all the juices.

For sausage & mixed bean stew, cook the potatoes as above. Fry the onions and peppers in the oil, then add 4 pork sausages instead of the chorizo. Cook for 4–5 minutes. Remove the sausages from the pan and cut each into 6 thick slices. Return to the pan, add the potato slices and tomatoes. Instead of the chickpeas add 400 g (13 oz) can mixed beans. Bring to the boil and cook as above. If you prefer a slightly hotter stew add 1 deseeded and chopped red chilli to the onions and peppers.

fillet steak with roquefort

Serves **4**

Preparation time **5 minutes**

Cooking time **7–10 minutes**

1 tablespoon crushed **peppercorns**

1 teaspoon **crushed dried chillies** (optional)

4 **fillet steaks**, at least 2.5 cm (1 inch) thick, about 175 g (6 oz) each

3 tablespoons **vegetable oil**

2 tablespoons **creamed horseradish**

175 g (6 oz) **Roquefort cheese**, crumbled

½ tablespoon chopped **flat leaf parsley**, plus extra to garnish

root vegetables, to serve

Mix together the crushed peppercorns and the crushed dried chillies, if using, on a plate. Press one side of each steak into the mixture to create a light crust.

Heat the oil in a large frying pan until very hot, then add the steaks, crust downwards. Sear on both sides until golden brown. Turn the steaks peppercorn crust upwards.

Mix the creamed horseradish and Roquefort together with the chopped parsley and spoon on to the top of each steak.

Cook the steaks for 2 more minutes for medium or 4–5 minutes for well-done meat. Then place briefly under a preheated hot grill to brown the Roquefort crust slightly. Garnish with extra parsley and serve immediately with root vegetables, such as sweet potatoes and beetroot.

pork with apples & mustard mash

Serves **4**
Preparation time **5 minutes**
Cooking time **23 minutes**

4 medium floury **potatoes**,
  diced
a handful **sage leaves**,
  chopped
2 tablespoons **extra virgin
  olive oil**
1 tablespoon **lemon juice**
1 tablespoon **clear honey**
1 large green **apple**, peeled,
  cored and quartered
1 **leek**, sliced
4 **pork steaks**, about 200 g
  (7 oz) each
50 g (2 oz) **butter**
2 tablespoons **milk**
1 tablespoon **Dijon mustard**
salt and **pepper**

Cook the potatoes in lightly salted boiling water for
10 minutes, until tender.

Meanwhile, mix the sage with the oil, lemon juice and
honey and season with salt and pepper. Mix half the
flavoured oil with the apple wedges and set aside.
Brush the rest over the pork.

Grill the steaks under a preheated hot grill for
3–4 minutes on each side, until browned and cooked
through. Set aside and keep warm.

Drain the potatoes, mash and beat in 40 g (1½ oz)
of the butter, the milk and mustard and season to
taste with salt and pepper. Keep warm.

Melt the remaining butter in a frying pan and quickly
fry the apple wedges with the leek for 2–3 minutes,
until golden and softened. Serve the pork with the
mustard mash, apples, leek and any pork juices.

For lamb with apricots & mustard mash, cook the
potatoes and make the mustard mash as above.
Instead of the sage, combine a handful of rosemary
with the oil, lemon juice, honey and salt and pepper.
Mix half this mixture with 125 g (4 oz) halved ready-to-
eat dried apricots. Brush the remaining mixture
over 4 lamb loin steaks and grill as above. Stir-fry the
apricot mixture in butter for 1 minute to warm through.
Serve the loin steaks on the mustard mash with the
warm apricots spooned over and with any remaining
juices from the pan.

fish & seafood

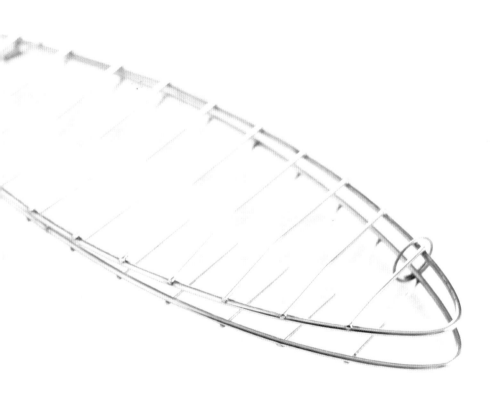

spicy tuna fishcakes

Serves **4**
Preparation time **10 minutes**
Cooking time **20 minutes**

250 g (8 oz) floury **potatoes**,
    peeled and cut into cubes
400 g (13 oz) can **tuna**,
    drained and flaked
50 g (2 oz) **Cheddar cheese**,
    grated
4 **spring onions**, finely
    chopped
1 small **garlic clove**, crushed
2 teaspoons **dried thyme**
1 small **egg**, beaten
½ teaspoon **cayenne pepper**
4 teaspoons **seasoned flour**
vegetable oil, for frying
salt and **pepper**

to serve
lemon wedges
watercress

Cook the potatoes in lightly salted boiling water for
10 minutes, until tender. Drain, mash and set aside to
cool down.

Beat the tuna, Cheddar, spring onions, garlic, thyme
and egg into the mashed potato, add the cayenne
pepper and season with salt and pepper.

Divide the mixture into 8 and make into thick burgers.
Sprinkle the flour over them and fry in a shallow layer
of hot oil for 5 minutes on each side, until they are
crisp and golden. Serve with lemon wedges and
watercress.

For salmon fishcakes, drain and flake 400 g (13 oz)
canned salmon. Cook the potatoes as above. Mix in
the salmon together with the spring onions, garlic,
egg, 50 g (2 oz) grated mozzarella cheese (instead
of Cheddar) and 4 tablespoons fresh chopped dill
(instead of thyme). Cook as above, then serve with
mayonnaise mixed with finely grated lemon rind and
chopped dill.

salmon with courgettes

Serves **4**
Preparation time **5 minutes**
Cooking time **15–20 minutes**

4 **salmon fillets**, about 150 g
   (5 oz) each
1 tablespoon prepared
   English mustard
1 teaspoon grated fresh **root
   ginger**
1 teaspoon crushed **garlic**
2 teaspoons **clear honey**
1 tablespoon **light soy sauce**
   or **tamari**

Lime courgettes
500 g (1 lb) **courgettes**, thinly
   sliced lengthways
2 tablespoons **olive oil**
grated rind and juice of
   1 lime
2 tablespoons chopped **mint**
salt and **pepper**

Place the portions of salmon fillet, skin side down, in a shallow flameproof dish. The portions should fit snugly in a single layer. Mix the mustard, ginger, garlic, honey and soy sauce or tamari together in a bowl, then spoon this mixture evenly over the fillets. Set aside.

Heat a ridged frying pan, put the courgettes and oil into a plastic bag and toss together, lift out the courgette slices and fry until lightly browned on each side and tender. You may need to do this in batches. Stir the lime rind and juice, mint and seasoning together in a bowl.

While the courgettes are cooking, heat the grill on the hottest setting. Grill the salmon fillets for 10–15 minutes, depending on their thickness, until lightly charred on top and cooked through. Transfer to serving plates, arrange the courgette slices around them and drizzle with the lime dressing. Serve hot.

For easy salmon en papillote, make the mustard topping and add to 4 salmon fillets as above. Slice 250 g (8 oz) courgettes and combine with 125 g (4 oz) asparagus tips and 125 g (4 oz) cherry tomatoes. Add the lime rind and juice and mint and place spoonfuls of the mixture in the centres of 4 pieces of foil. Place the mustard-crusted salmon fillets over the top. Wrap the salmon in the foil, leaving a gap for air to escape, and bake in a preheated oven, 200°C (400°F), Gas Mark 6, for 20 minutes until the fish is opaque and cooked through and the vegetables are tender. Serve immediately.

blackened cod with salsa

Serves **4**
Preparation time **15 minutes**
Cooking time **8 minutes**

1 large **orange**
1 **garlic clove**, crushed
2 large **tomatoes**, skinned,
 deseeded and diced
2 tablespoons chopped **basil**
50 g (2 oz) pitted **black
 olives**, chopped
5 tablespoons **extra virgin
 olive oil**
4 thick **cod fillets**, about
 175 g (6 oz) each
1 tablespoon **jerk seasoning**
salt and **pepper**
rocket leaves, to serve

Peel and segment the orange, holding it over a bowl to catch the juices. Halve the segments. Mix them with the garlic, tomatoes, basil, olives and 4 tablespoons of the oil, season to taste with salt and pepper and set the salsa aside to infuse.

Wash and pat dry the fish and pull out any small bones with a pair of tweezers. Brush with the remaining oil and coat well with the jerk seasoning.

Heat a large heavy-based frying pan and fry the cod fillets, skin side down, for 5 minutes. Turn them over and cook for a further 3 minutes. Transfer to a low oven, 150°C (300°F), Gas Mark 2, to rest for about 5 minutes.

Serve the fish with the salsa and some rocket leaves.

For spiced cod with avocado & tomato salsa,
instead of jerk seasoning, rub $1/2$ teaspoon Cajun spice over each of 4 cod fillets. Make the salsa by chopping 1 ripe avocado and 2 large tomatoes and combining with the finely grated rind and juice of 1 lime and plenty of seasoning. Omit the orange, garlic, basil, black olives and olive oil. Cook the cod as above and serve with the salsa spooned over.

grilled spiced cod

Serves **4**
Preparation time **10 minutes**,
  plus marinating
Cooking time **20 minutes**

4 thick **cod loin** or **halibut
  steaks**, about 175 g (6 oz)
  each
1 **red onion**, thinly sliced
2 **garlic cloves**, crushed
2 teaspoons grated fresh **root
  ginger**
1 teaspoon **cumin seeds**,
  roughly crushed
1 teaspoon **ground coriander**
1 teaspoon **crushed dried
  chillies**
½ teaspoon **turmeric**
juice of 3 **limes** or 2 **lemons**
4 tablespoons **olive oil**
salt and **pepper**

To serve
lime or **lemon wedges**
rice

Put the fish steaks into a large, china dish.

Add the onion, garlic, ginger, cumin, ground coriander,
chilli and turmeric to a bowl. Add the lime or lemon
juice and oil, season with salt and pepper and
mix together.

Spoon the onion marinade over the fish, using your
hands to coat the fish thoroughly on both sides. Cover
and marinate in the refrigerator for 3–4 hours.

Preheat the grill and line the rack with foil. Transfer the
fish, skin side down, and marinade to the foil and then
grill for 8–10 minutes until the fish is lightly browned
and flakes easily when pressed with a knife. Serve with
lime or lemon wedges and rice.

For halibut curry, make the sauce as above and add
500 ml (17 fl oz) natural yogurt and 150 ml (¼ pint)
double cream. Cut 750 g (1½ lb) halibut into bite-
sized chunks and marinate in the spicy yogurt and
cream mixture for 1 hour. Transfer all the ingredients
to a large pan and bring to a steady boil. As soon as
it boils, reduce the heat to a simmer and gently stir
once or twice, then simmer for 5 minutes, adding a
large handful of chopped fresh coriander leaves for
the final 1 minute of cooking. Serve with rice or warm
naan bread.

fish casserole

Serves **4**
Preparation time **10 minutes**
Cooking time **15 minutes**

3 tablespoons **olive oil**
2 **red onions**, finely diced
2 **garlic cloves**, crushed
½ teaspoon **crushed dried chillies**
200 g (7 oz) **squid**, cleaned and cut into thin strips, tentacles reserved
200 g (7 oz) **mussels**, scrubbed and debearded
200 g (7 oz) **clams**, cleaned or extra mussels if clams are unavailable
300 g (10 oz) **king prawns** in their shells
150 ml (¼ pint) **fish stock**
150 ml (¼ pint) dry **white wine**
½ teaspoon **saffron**
8 **tomatoes**, skinned and deseeded
1 **bay leaf**
1 teaspoon **sugar**
400 g (13 oz) **red mullet** or **sea bass fillets**, cut into bite-sized pieces
salt and **pepper**
green salad, to serve

Heat the oil in a saucepan large enough to hold all the ingredients. Add the onions and garlic and sauté gently for 5 minutes. Add the crushed dried chillies and mix well.

Add the squid, mussels, clams and king prawns and stir well.

Add the stock, wine, saffron, tomatoes, bay leaf and sugar and season with salt and pepper. Cover the pan and simmer gently for 5 minutes. Discard any mussels or clams that do not open.

Add the red mullet or sea bass and simmer for a further 5 minutes, then serve at once with a green salad.

For a creamy fish casserole, cook 2 white onions (not red ones) as above with the garlic and chilli and add 1 bunch of sliced spring onions. Add the seafood as above, stir in the stock, wine, saffron, bay leaf and sugar, omitting the tomatoes, and bring to the boil. Season to taste, simmer for 5 minutes to reduce the wine by half, then add 200 ml (7 fl oz) crème fraîche and 300 ml (½ pint) double cream. Continue to cook for a further 5 minutes. Blend 1 tablespoon cornflour with 2 tablespoons water and add to the casserole with the parsley and finely grated rind of 1 lemon. Stir well until slightly thickened. Serve with rice and a simple salad.

prawns in chillied tomato soup

Serves **4**

Preparation time **10 minutes**

Cooking time **10–12 minutes**

2 tablespoons **olive oil**

2 **red onions**, finely chopped

3 **garlic cloves**, crushed

1 **red chilli**, deseeded and chopped

2 strips of **lemon rind**

2 large, ripe, well-flavoured **tomatoes**

150 ml (¼ pint) **fish stock**

500 g (1 lb) peeled raw **tiger prawns**

salt and **pepper**

2 tablespoons chopped mixed **parsley** and **dill**, to garnish

Heat the oil in a heavy-based frying pan. Add the onions, garlic, chilli and lemon rind and fry over a medium heat, stirring occasionally, for 1–2 minutes. Add the tomatoes and stock and bring to the boil. Lower the heat and simmer for 5 minutes.

Add the prawns, season to taste with salt and pepper and cook, turning occasionally, for about 4 minutes, until the prawns are pink. Garnish with the mixed herbs and serve immediately.

For white fish & vegetable stew, trim and roughly chop 2 large courgettes. Cook the onions, garlic and chilli as above, add the courgettes and cook for 1–2 minutes. Add 250 g (8 oz) peeled prawns and 250 g (8 oz) firm white fish, such as monkfish or cod. Stir in 125 g (4 oz) black olives and 5 tablespoons chopped parsley and cook as above. Serve with warm crusty granary bread.

griddled tuna salad

Serves **4**
Preparation time **10 minutes**
Cooking time **15 minutes**

500 g (1 lb) small **new potatoes**, scrubbed
4 fresh **tuna steaks**, about 175 g (6 oz) each
100 g (3½ oz) **baby spinach leaves**, roughly chopped
4 tablespoons **olive oil**
2 tablespoons **balsamic vinegar**
salt and **pepper**
griddled **lime wedges**, to serve

Place the new potatoes in a steamer over boiling water and cook for 15 minutes or until tender.

Meanwhile, heat a griddle pan. Pat the tuna fillets dry with kitchen paper and cook in the pan for 3 minutes on each side for rare, 5 minutes for medium or 8 minutes for well done.

Remove the potatoes from the steamer. Slice them in half and place in a bowl. Add the spinach, olive oil and balsamic vinegar. Toss and season to taste. Divide the salad between 4 plates and serve with a slice of tuna arranged on the top of each, and a griddled lime wedge for squeezing.

For warm niçoise salad, cook the potatoes and tuna as above. Halve and blanch 125 g (4 oz) fine beans and quickly fry 125 g (4 oz) cherry tomatoes. Add the beans and tomatoes and 125 g (4 oz) black olives to the halved warm potatoes and spinach leaves. Flake the tuna and add to the salad. Season well and serve.

five-spice salmon

Serves **4**
Preparation time **5 minutes**
Cooking time **12 minutes**

2 teaspoons crushed **pepper**
2 teaspoons **Chinese five-spice powder**
1 teaspoon **salt**
large pinch of **cayenne pepper**
4 **salmon fillets**, about 175 g (6 oz) each, skinned
3 tablespoons **sunflower oil**
500 g (1 lb) **choi sum** or **pak choi**, sliced
3 **garlic cloves**, sliced
3 tablespoons **shao hsing** (Chinese rice wine) or **dry sherry**
75 ml (3 fl oz) **vegetable stock**
2 tablespoons **light soy sauce**
1 teaspoon **sesame oil**
rice, to serve

Combine the pepper, five-spice powder, salt and cayenne pepper in a small bowl. Brush the salmon with a little of the oil and dust with the spice coating. Cook the fish in a preheated frying pan for 4 minutes, then turn and cook for a further 2–3 minutes until the fish is just cooked through. Transfer to a plate, cover with foil and leave to rest for 5 minutes.

Meanwhile, heat the remaining oil in a wok, add the choi sum or pak choi and stir-fry for 2 minutes, then add the garlic and stir-fry for a further 1 minute. Add the shao hsing or sherry, stock, soy sauce and sesame oil and cook for a further 2 minutes until the greens are tender.

Serve the salmon and greens with boiled rice.

For stir-fried spicy salmon, prepare the spice mixture as above. Cut the salmon into chunks and toss in a bowl with the spice mixture to coat. Heat 1 tablespoon oil in a frying pan and cook the salmon for 3–4 minutes, taking care not to break it up too much. Remove the salmon from the pan with a slotted spoon and keep warm. Add 2 tablespoons oil to the pan and stir-fry the pak choi with 125 g (4 oz) mangetout or sugar snap peas and 125 g (4 oz) thin julienne carrot strips for 2 minutes before adding the rice wine or sherry, soy sauce, stock and sesame oil. Return the salmon to the pan, stir carefully to combine and heat through. Serve immediately.

trout with pesto

Serves **4**
Preparation time **10 minutes**
Cooking time **10 minutes**

4 tablespoons **olive oil**, plus
    extra for greasing
4 **trout fillets**, about 200 g
    (7 oz) each
large handful of **basil**, roughly
    chopped, plus extra to
    garnish
1 **garlic clove**, crushed
50 g (2 oz) **Parmesan
    cheese**, freshly grated
salt and **pepper**
salad, to serve

Brush a baking sheet lightly with oil and place under
a preheated very hot grill to heat up.

Put the trout fillets on to the hot sheet, sprinkle with
salt and pepper and place under the grill for 8–10
minutes until lightly browned and the fish flakes easily
when pressed with a knife.

Meanwhile, put the basil and garlic into a bowl. Work
in the oil using a hand-held blender. Stir in the
Parmesan cheese.

Remove the fish from the grill, transfer to serving
plates, drizzle with the pesto, sprinkle with extra basil
leaves to garnish and serve with salad.

For orange & almond trout, put the trout fillets on
a foil-lined grill rack as above. Mix together the finely
grated rind and juice of 1 small orange, 1 tablespoon
chopped parsley and 4 tablespoons olive oil. Brush
the mixture over the fillets and season with salt and
pepper. Grill until golden and opaque, then sprinkle
with toasted flaked almonds. Serve with fresh crusty
granary bread and a simple salad.

cod & olive risotto

Serves **4**
Preparation time **10 minutes**
Cooking time **25 minutes**

500 g (1 lb) **cod fillet**, skinned
600 ml (1 pint) **white wine**
600 ml (1 pint) hot **fish stock**
50 g (2 oz) **butter**
2 **onions**, chopped
375 g (12 oz) **risotto rice**
50 g (2 oz) **sun-dried
  tomatoes** in oil, drained and
  sliced
4 tablespoons **olive oil**
2 tablespoons chopped
  oregano
200 g (7 oz) **cherry
  tomatoes**, halved
50 g (2 oz) **Parmesan
  cheese**, freshly grated
50 g (2 oz) pitted **black
  olives**, chopped
1 tablespoon **white wine
  vinegar**
salt and **pepper**

Pat the fish dry on kitchen paper and cut into 4 pieces. Season with salt and pepper. Put the wine and stock in a saucepan and bring almost to the boil. Set aside.

Melt the butter in a large, heavy-based saucepan and sauté the onions for 5 minutes, until softened. Add the rice and sun-dried tomatoes and stir well to coat the grains with the butter. Add the hot stock mixture, a large ladleful at a time, stirring until each addition is absorbed into the rice. Continue adding stock in this way, cooking until the rice is creamy but the grains are still firm. This should take about 20 minutes.

Meanwhile, heat 2 tablespoons of the oil in a large frying pan and cook the fish for 3 minutes on each side, until cooked through. Remove with a fish slice and keep warm.

Add the oregano and tomatoes to the pan and cook for 1 minute. Season lightly with salt and pepper.

Stir the Parmesan into the risotto and pile on to plates. Top with the fish and tomatoes. Add the olives, the remaining oil and the vinegar to the frying pan, stirring for a few seconds, then pour over the fish to serve.

For prawn & pea risotto, cook the onions in butter as above. Add the rice and cook, then add the stock as above. When the rice has absorbed almost all the stock and it is tender, add 250 g (8 oz) prawns, 175 g (6 oz) frozen peas and 6 tablespoons chopped mint. Heat for 5 minutes with the final ladleful of stock. Stir in the Parmesan cheese and 200 ml (7 fl oz) crème fraîche. Heat for a further minute before serving in warm serving bowls with plenty of pepper.

swordfish with sage pangritata

Serves **4**
Preparation time **5 minutes**
Cooking time **6 minutes**

5 tablespoons **extra virgin
    olive oil**, plus extra to serve
2 **garlic cloves**, chopped
2 tablespoons chopped **sage
    leaves**
125 g (4 oz) **fresh white
    breadcrumbs**
grated rind and juice of
    1 lemon
250 g (8 oz) fine **green beans**
4 **swordfish fillets**, about
    200 g (7 oz) each

Heat 4 tablespoons of the oil in a frying pan and fry
the garlic, sage, breadcrumbs and lemon rind, stirring
constantly, for 5 minutes until crisp and golden. Drain
the pangritata thoroughly on kitchen paper.

Cook the beans in a pan of lightly salted boiling water
for 3 minutes until just tender. Drain well, season with
salt and pepper and toss with a little of the lemon juice.
Keep warm.

Meanwhile, brush the swordfish with the remaining oil,
season with salt and pepper and sear in a preheated
griddle pan for 1½ minutes on each side. Remove from
the pan, cover with foil and rest briefly.

Transfer the swordfish to plates, drizzle with the
remaining lemon juice and top with the pangritata.
Place the beans alongside and drizzle with oil.

For smoky bacon swordfish with creamy leeks,
lightly fry the garlic, sage, breadcrumbs and lemon
rind as above with 3 finely chopped streaky bacon
rashers. When the bacon is crisp and golden remove
the mixture from the pan and drain on kitchen paper.
Instead of the green beans chop 250 g (8 oz) leeks,
add them to the pan and cook for 3 minutes. Drain
and toss with 200 ml (7 fl oz) crème fraîche mixed
with ¹/₂ teaspoon Dijon mustard. Cook the swordfish
as above and serve it on a bed of leeks with the
bacon and sage breadcrumbs scattered over the top.

tuna with sun-dried tomatoes

Serves **4**
Preparation time **5 minutes**
Cooking time **10–15 minutes**

3 tablespoons **olive oil**
1 **red onion**, finely chopped
2 **garlic cloves**, crushed
1 **rosemary sprig**, chopped
3 tablespoons **plain flour**
4 fresh **tuna steaks**, about
    175 g (6 oz) each
125 g (4 oz) **sun-dried
    tomatoes**, in oil, drained
    and chopped
75 ml (3 fl oz) **red wine**
1 tablespoon **capers** in brine,
    drained
75 g (3 oz) pitted **black olives**
handful of **flat leaf parsley**,
    chopped
salt and **pepper**

To serve
lemon wedges
crusty bread

Heat 2 tablespoons of the oil in a saucepan, add
the onion, garlic and rosemary and sauté gently for
5 minutes.

Season the flour with salt and pepper. Dip the tuna
into the flour to coat evenly.

Heat the remaining oil in a frying pan, add the tuna
and cook for 2–3 minutes or until golden. Turn over
and cook on the other side for a further 1–3 minutes
or longer, according to taste. Transfer to a dish lined
with kitchen paper and keep warm in the oven.

Add the sun-dried tomatoes to the sautéed onions and
stir well. Turn up the heat to high, add the wine, capers,
olives and parsley and season with salt and pepper.
Simmer for 2 minutes. Serve the sauce with the tuna
steaks, lemon wedges and crusty bread.

For tuna & sun-dried tomato pilaff, cook the tuna
steaks as above. Flake the flesh into large pieces
and set aside. Cook 175 g (6 oz) brown basmati
rice, drain and set aside. Cook the onion, garlic and
rosemary as above and add the chopped sun-dried
tomatoes. Add the rice and stir-fry together. Add
125 g (4 oz) shredded mangetout and cook for
1 minute. Add the wine, capers, olives and parsley
and return the flaked tuna to the pan. Cook for a
further 2 minutes, stirring occasionally and taking
care not to break up the fish too much. Serve hot
with a simple dressed green salad.

monkfish kebabs

Serves **4**

Preparation time **10 minutes**, plus marinating

Cooking time **8–10 minutes**

1 kg (2 lb) **monkfish fillet**, cut into 4 cm (1½ inch) cubes

200 ml (7 fl oz) **natural yogurt**

4 tablespoons **lemon juice**

3 **garlic cloves**, crushed

2 teaspoons grated fresh **root ginger**

1 teaspoon **hot chilli powder**

1 teaspoon **ground cumin**

1 teaspoon **ground coriander**

2 **Thai red chillies**, finely sliced

salt and **pepper**

To serve
salad
naan bread

Put the monkfish into a non-metallic bowl.

Mix together the yogurt, lemon juice, garlic, ginger, chilli powder, cumin, ground coriander and chillies in a small bowl, and season with salt and pepper. Pour this over the fish, cover and marinate in the refrigerator for 3–4 hours or overnight if time allows.

Lift the fish out of the marinade and thread on to 8 flat metal skewers. Place on a grill rack and cook under a preheated hot grill for 8–10 minutes, turning once, until the fish is cooked through. Serve hot, with salad and naan bread.

For chilli monkfish, potato & coriander curry,

make the marinade as above and add an additional 1 teaspoon garam masala to the spices. Halve 250 g (8 oz) new potatoes and cook until tender. Transfer the potatoes to a large saucepan with the fish and marinade. Add 150 ml (¼ pint) fish stock, bring to a simmer and cook for 10 minutes or until the fish is opaque and cooked through. Stir in a large bunch of roughly chopped fresh coriander. Serve with rice and naan bread.

sesame steamed prawns

Serves **4**
Preparation time **15 minutes**
Cooking time **5 minutes**

300 g (10 oz) raw **tiger
  prawns**, peeled, with tails
  intact, defrosted if frozen
2 **garlic cloves**, sliced
1 **red chilli**, deseeded and
  chopped
grated rind and juice of
  1 lime
2.5 cm (1 inch) piece of fresh
  root ginger, peeled and
  chopped
2 tablespoons **rice wine**
2 tablespoons **Thai fish
  sauce**
4 **Savoy cabbage leaves**
1 tablespoon **sesame oil**
salt
mixed fresh herbs, such as
  coriander, mint and basil,
  to garnish

Rinse the prawns with cold water, drain and pat dry.

Mix the garlic, chilli, lime rind and juice, ginger, rice wine and fish sauce in a bowl. Add the prawns and toss well. Set aside.

Blanch the cabbage leaves in lightly salted boiling water for 30 seconds, then drain and refresh under cold water. Pat dry.

Arrange the cabbage leaves in a bamboo steamer and carefully spoon the prawns and their marinade on top of the leaves. Cover and steam for 2–3 minutes, until the prawns are pink.

Place the cabbage leaves and prawns on a serving dish. Heat the sesame oil in a small saucepan and pour it over them, then garnish with the herbs.

For crab & prawn parcels, mix together the garlic, chilli, lime rind and juice, ginger, rice wine and fish sauce. Add 1 thinly sliced lemon grass stalk. Drain 200 g (7 oz) canned crab and mix with 125 g (4 oz) small cooked prawns. Toss the seafood with the marinade ingredients. Spoon the mixture on to 8 cabbage leaves and roll them into parcels, folding the sides in and over to contain the filling. Secure with a cocktail stick in each. Steam as above and serve warm with sweet chilli sauce.

sea bass with spicy salsa

Serves **4**

Preparation time **15 minutes**, plus standing

Cooking time **6–8 minutes**

4 **sea bass fillets**, about 175 g (6 oz) each

2 tablespoons **olive oil**

parsley sprigs, to garnish

Spicy salsa

4 **plum tomatoes**, skinned, deseeded and roughly chopped

1 **red chilli**, finely chopped

2 **garlic cloves**, finely chopped

50 g (2 oz) pitted **black olives**, finely chopped

1 **shallot**, finely chopped

4 tablespoons **olive oil**

4 tablespoons **lemon juice**

salt and **pepper**

To serve

tagliatelle

spinach salad

lemon wedges

Place all the spicy salsa ingredients in a large bowl. Mix well and set aside for at least 1 hour to allow the flavours to blend.

Heat a griddle pan, brush the sea bass fillets with oil and fry for 3–4 minutes on each side. Serve garnished with parsley on a bed of tagliatelle with the spicy salsa, a spinach salad and some lemon wedges.

For sea bass with lime salsa & spicy chips, make the salsa as above but add the finely grated rind of 1 lime. Cook the sea bass fillets as above. Make spicy chips by cutting 4 large baking potatoes into thin wedges and toss in 4 tablespoons olive oil. Roast in a preheated oven, 200°C (400°F), Gas Mark 6, for 20 minutes before sprinkling with 1 teaspoon flaky salt and 1 teaspoon Cajun spice. Toss well, return to the oven and cook for a further 10 minutes until golden and crisp in places. Serve the fish with the chips and salsa on the side.

vegetables

vegetable bolognese

Serves **4**
Preparation time **10 minutes**
Cooking time **15 minutes**

½ tablespoon **vegetable oil**
1 **onion**, chopped
200 g (7 oz) can **baby carrots**, drained and chopped
1 **leek**, sliced
2 **celery sticks**, sliced
400 g (13 oz) can **chopped tomatoes**
1 tablespoon **tomato purée**
1 teaspoon **cayenne pepper**
125 g (4 oz) **mushrooms**, sliced
375 g (12 oz) **spaghetti**
salt and **pepper**
basil leaves, to garnish

Heat the oil in a saucepan. Add the onion and fry over a low heat for 3–5 minutes, until soft. Stir in the carrots, leek and celery, then the tomatoes, tomato purée, cayenne pepper and mushrooms. Add a pinch of salt and pepper and simmer for 10 minutes.

Meanwhile, cook the spaghetti in a saucepan of lightly salted boiling water for 8–10 minutes, or according to the packet instructions, until al dente. Drain the pasta and sprinkle with pepper. To serve, mound up the spaghetti and spoon the sauce over the top. Garnish with basil leaves.

For vegetarian bolognese, peel and grate 2 large carrots. Heat the oil in a pan and fry the onion as above. Add 250 g (8 oz) minced texture vegetable soya protein (quorn mince) and the grated carrots, 1 sliced leek and 2 chopped celery sticks. Fry for 3–4 minutes, then add the tomatoes, tomato purée, cayenne and mushrooms. Simmer for 10 minutes as above. Ladle over the cooked and drained spaghetti and top with plenty of grated Parmesan cheese. Serve with garlic bread.

mushroom toad-in-the-hole

Serves **4**
Preparation time **5 minutes**
Cooking time **25–30 minutes**

4 large or 400 g (13 oz)
   smaller **open mushrooms**
25 g (1 oz) **butter**
5 tablespoons **olive oil**
3 **garlic cloves**, sliced
2 tablespoons chopped
   rosemary or **thyme**
125 g (4 oz) **plain flour**
2 **eggs**
2 tablespoons **horseradish**
   sauce
400 ml (14 fl oz) **milk**
salt and **pepper**

Beer gravy
2 **onions**, sliced
2 teaspoons **sugar**
1 tablespoon **plain flour**
275 ml (9 fl oz) **beer**
150 ml (¼ pint) **vegetable**
   stock

Heat the oven to 230°C (450°F), Gas Mark 8.

Put the mushrooms, stalk side up, in a large, shallow ovenproof dish.

Melt the butter with 4 tablespoons of the oil in a frying pan. Add the garlic and herbs and a little salt and pepper and stir for about 30 seconds. Pour the sauce over the mushrooms and bake in the oven for 2 minutes.

Meanwhile, put the flour in a bowl and slowly whisk in the eggs, horseradish sauce, milk and a little salt and pepper until really smooth.

Pour the batter over the mushrooms and return to the oven for 20–25 minutes, until the batter has risen and is golden.

Heat the rest of the oil in a frying pan. Add the onions and sugar and fry for 10 minutes until deep golden, stir in the flour, then pour in the beer and stock and add a sprinkling of salt and pepper. Stir for 5 minutes.

Cut up the toad and pour the beer gravy generously over the top of each serving.

For vegetable toad-in-the-hole, trim and peel 2 large carrots and 2 large parsnips. Cut them in half lengthways and then into 5 cm (2 inch) pieces. Trim 2 courgettes and cut them into 5 cm (2 inch) pieces. Heat the butter and oil in the frying pan and cook the vegetables for 2–3 minutes over a moderately high heat. Add the garlic and rosemary and cook for a further 1 minute. Continue as above, replacing the mushrooms with the vegetables. Serve with the gravy

stuffed aubergines

Serves **4**
Preparation time **15 minutes**
Cooking time **25 minutes**

2 **aubergines**
4 tablespoons **olive oil**, plus
    extra for oiling
8 **tomatoes**, skinned and
    chopped
2 **garlic cloves**, crushed
4 **anchovy fillets** in oil,
    drained and chopped
1 tablespoon **capers**,
    chopped
handful of **basil**, chopped,
    plus extra to garnish
handful of **flat leaf parsley**,
    chopped, plus extra to
    garnish
2 tablespoons **pine nuts**,
    toasted
50 g (2 oz) **fresh white
    breadcrumbs**
75 g (3 oz) **pecorino cheese**,
    grated
salt and **pepper**

Cut the aubergines in half lengthways and scoop out the flesh without breaking the skin. Roughly chop the flesh.

Heat the oil in a frying pan. Add the aubergine shells and sauté them on each side for 3–4 minutes. Place them in a lightly oiled baking dish. Add the aubergine flesh to the pan and sauté until golden brown.

Mix the tomatoes, garlic, anchovies, capers, basil, parsley, pine nuts, breadcrumbs, aubergine flesh and half of the pecorino together and season with salt and pepper. Spoon the mixture into the sautéed aubergine shells, piling it high. Sprinkle with the remaining cheese. Place in a preheated oven, 200°C (400°F), Gas Mark 6, and cook for 20 minutes. Serve sprinkled with extra chopped herbs.

For cashew & raisin filled aubergines, prepare the aubergines as above. Fry the chopped aubergine flesh with 3 roughly chopped sun-dried tomatoes, 75 g (3 oz) cashew nuts, 75 g (3 oz) raisins and a handful of chopped flat leaf parsley over a high heat for 3–4 minutes or until the aubergine is golden and soft. Pile the mixture into the aubergine shells and sprinkle over 50 g (2 oz) chopped mozzarella cheese. Bake in the oven as above for 20 minutes and serve with a simple rocket salad.

haloumi with paprika oil

Serves **4**
Preparation time **5 minutes**
Cooking time **5 minutes**

6 tablespoons **extra virgin
  olive oil**
4 tablespoons **lemon juice**
½ teaspoon **smoked paprika**
250 g (8 oz) **haloumi cheese**,
  cut into chunks
salt and **pepper**

Combine the oil, lemon juice and paprika in a small bowl and season the mixture with salt and pepper.

Heat a heavy-based frying pan until hot, then add the haloumi and toss over a medium heat until golden and starting to soften. Transfer immediately to a plate, drizzle over the paprika oil and serve with cocktail sticks to spike the haloumi.

For chilli & tomato jam to serve with the haloumi, heat 1 tablespoon of oil in a pan and add 1 finely chopped red chilli, 1 finely chopped shallot, 3 tablespoons sugar and 4 roughly chopped tomatoes. Season well with salt and pepper and cook over a moderately high heat for 15 minutes, stirring occasionally until thick, pulpy and soft. Remove from the heat and allow to cool. Serve with griddled haloumi.

mushroom & spinach lasagne

Serves **4**
Preparation time **20 minutes**
Cooking time **25–30 minutes**

250 g (8 oz) pack of 6 **fresh
lasagne sheets**
3 tablespoons **olive oil**
500 g (1 lb) **mixed
mushrooms** such as
shiitake, oyster and chestnut,
sliced
2 **garlic cloves**, finely
chopped
200 g (7 oz) **mascarpone
cheese**
125 g (4 oz) **baby spinach
leaves**
150 g (5 oz) **taleggio cheese**,
derinded and cut into cubes
salt and **pepper**

Place the lasagne sheets in a large roasting tray and cover with boiling water. Leave to stand for 5 minutes, or until tender, then drain off the water.

Heat the oil in a large frying pan and fry the mushrooms for 5 minutes. Add the garlic and mascarpone and turn up the heat. Cook for another 1 minute until the sauce is thick. Season with salt and pepper. Steam the spinach for 2 minutes or microwave until just wilted.

Oil an ovenproof dish about the size of 2 of the lasagne sheets and place 2 of the lasagne sheets over the base, slightly overlapping. Reserve one-third of the taleggio for the top, sprinkle a little over the pasta base with one third of the mushroom sauce and one-third of the spinach leaves. Repeat with 2 more layers, topping the final layer of lasagne sheets with the remaining mushroom sauce, spinach and taleggio.

Bake in a preheated oven, 200°C (400°F), Gas Mark 6, for 15–20 minutes until the cheese is golden and the lasagne piping hot.

For walnut, spinach & squash lasagne, prepare the lasagne and spinach as above. Heat 3 tablespoons oil in a frying pan and cook 500 g (1 lb) roughly chopped butternut squash. Add the garlic and mascarpone, season to taste and add $1/2$ teaspoon paprika. Mix in 125 g (4 oz) finely chopped walnuts and cook for a further minute. Assemble the lasagne, layering the squash sauce and spinach and topping with taleggio cheese as above. Bake in a preheated oven, 200°C (400°F) Gas Mark 6, for 25 minutes until golden.

couscous with grilled vegetables

Serves **4**
Preparation time **15 minutes**,
  plus standing
Cooking time **10 minutes**

300 g (10 oz) **couscous**
500 ml (17 fl oz) boiling **water**
2 **red peppers**, cored,
  deseeded and quartered
1 **orange** or **yellow pepper**,
  cored, deseeded and
  quartered
6 **baby courgettes**, halved
  lengthways
2 **red onions**, cut into wedges
24 **cherry tomatoes**
2 **garlic cloves**, finely sliced
2 tablespoons **olive oil**
100 g (3½ oz) **asparagus**,
  trimmed
grated rind and juice of
  1 lemon
4 tablespoons chopped
  parsley or **mint**
salt and **pepper**
lemon wedges, to serve

Tip the couscous into a large heatproof bowl, pour over the measurement boiling water, cover and set aside for 10 minutes.

Meanwhile, put the peppers, courgettes, onions, tomatoes and garlic into a grill pan in a single layer, drizzle over the oil and cook under a preheated hot grill for 5–6 minutes, turning occasionally.

Add the asparagus to the pan and continue to grill for 2–3 minutes until the vegetables are tender and lightly charred. When they are cool enough to handle, remove the skins from the peppers and discard.

Fork through the couscous to separate the grains. Toss with the vegetables, lemon rind and juice and herbs, season to taste with salt and pepper and serve immediately with lemon wedges.

For roasted vegetable couscous, prepare 300 g (10 oz) couscous by adding 500 ml (17 fl oz) boiling chicken stock. Roughly chop 500 g (1 lb) butternut squash, trim and chop 1 courgette, cut 6 plum tomatoes into quarters and halve and slice 1 fennel bulb. Toss the vegetables in 2 tablespoons oil and 2 sliced garlic cloves and roast in a preheated oven, 200°C (400°F), Gas Mark 6, for 25 minutes until lightly charred in places and soft. Stir 1 tablespoon honey through the vegetables. Toss the vegetables into the couscous with the lemon rind and parsley, season well and serve.

vegetable biryani

Serves **4**
Preparation time **10 minutes**
Cooking time **20 minutes**

250 g (8 oz) **long-grain rice**
2 tablespoons **olive oil**
3 **carrots**, chopped
2 medium **potatoes**, chopped
2.5 cm (1 inch) piece of fresh
  root ginger, peeled and
  grated
2 **garlic cloves**, crushed
200 g (7 oz) **cauliflower
  florets**
125 g (4 oz) **green beans**,
  halved
1 tablespoon **hot curry paste**
1 teaspoon **turmeric**
1 teaspoon **ground cinnamon**
250 g (8 oz) **natural yogurt**
40 g (1½ oz) **raisins**

To serve
75 g (3 oz) **cashew nuts**,
  toasted
2 tablespoons chopped fresh
  coriander leaves

Cook the rice according to the packet instructions and drain.

Meanwhile, heat the oil in a saucepan, add the carrots, potato, ginger and garlic and fry for 10 minutes until soft, adding a little water if the potatoes begin to stick.

Stir in the cauliflower, beans, curry paste, turmeric and cinnamon and cook for 1 minute. Stir in the yogurt and raisins.

Pile the rice on top of the vegetables, cover and cook over a low heat for 10 minutes, checking it isn't sticking to the pan.

Serve the biryani sprinkled with the cashew nuts and coriander.

For lamb biryani, prepare the rice as above. Cut 250 g (8 oz) lamb fillet into strips. Omitting the potatoes, cook the carrots, ginger and garlic as above together with the lamb for 10 minutes. Add the cauliflower, beans, curry paste and spices and 4 roughly chopped baby aubergines. Cook for 1 minute, then add the yogurt and raisins as above. Add to the rice and cook as above. Serve sprinkled with flaked almonds instead of cashew nuts and with extra yogurt, if liked.

artichoke & mozzarella pizza

Serves **4**
Preparation time **10 minutes**
Cooking time **15–20 minutes**

250 g (8 oz) **self-raising flour**
3 tablespoons **oil**
1 teaspoon **salt**
2 tablespoons **sun-dried tomato paste**
100 ml (3½ fl oz) **water**

Topping

1 tablespoon **sun-dried tomato paste**
2 large, mild **red chillies** or **green chillies**, halved and deseeded
3 tablespoons chopped **mixed fresh herbs**, such as parsley, oregano, rosemary and chives
50 g (2 oz) **sun-dried tomatoes** in oil, drained and sliced
150 g (5 oz) **baby artichokes** in oil, drained
2 **plum tomatoes**, cut into quarters
150 g (5 oz) **mozzarella cheese**, sliced
50 g (2 oz) pitted **black olives**
salt and **pepper**

Grease a large baking sheet. Place the flour in a bowl with the oil, salt and sun-dried tomato paste. Add the measurement water and mix to a soft dough, adding a little more water if necessary.

Roll out the dough on a lightly floured surface to a round about 28 cm (11 inches) in diameter. Place on the prepared baking sheet and bake in a preheated oven, 230°C (450°F), Gas Mark 8, for 5 minutes.

Spread the pizza base to within 1 cm (½ inch) of the edge with the sun-dried tomato paste. Cut the chillies in half lengthways again and scatter over the pizza with half the herbs, the sun-dried tomatoes, artichokes, tomatoes, mozzarella and olives. Scatter the remaining herbs on top and season lightly with salt and pepper.

Return the pizza to the oven and bake for 10–15 minutes until the cheese has melted and the vegetables are beginning to colour.

For egg & spinach pizza, make, roll out and bake a pizza base as above, using 250 g (8 oz) wholemeal flour instead of self-raising flour. Spread 4 tablespoons pasta sauce or pizza topping sauce over the base and scatter over 50 g (2 oz) blanched and squeezed spinach. Break an egg over the spinach and scatter over 2 tablespoons pine nuts. Bake as above until the egg is set and the dough has risen.

curried tofu burgers

Serves **4**
Preparation time **15 minutes**
Cooking time **10–15 minutes**

2 tablespoons **vegetable oil**
1 large **carrot**, coarsely grated
1 small **red onion**, finely
   chopped
1 **garlic clove**, crushed
1 teaspoon **hot curry paste**
1 teaspoon **sun-dried tomato
   paste**
250 g (8 oz) **firm tofu**,
   drained
25 g (1 oz) **fresh wholemeal
   breadcrumbs**
25 g (1 oz) **unsalted peanuts**,
   finely chopped
plain flour, for dusting
salt and **pepper**

To serve
4 **burger buns**
3 **tomatoes**, sliced
green salad leaves
alfalfa
tomato ketchup or **chillied
   tomato chutney**

Heat half the oil in a large nonstick frying pan
and fry the carrot and onion, stirring constantly, for
3–4 minutes, or until the vegetables are softened. Add
the garlic and curry and tomato pastes. Increase the
heat and fry for 2 minutes, stirring constantly.

Whizz the tofu, vegetables, breadcrumbs and peanuts
in a food processor or blender until just combined.
Transfer to a bowl, season well with salt and pepper
and beat until the mixture starts to stick together.

Shape the mixture into 4 burgers. Heat the remaining
oil in a large nonstick frying pan and fry the burgers
for 3–4 minutes on each side, or until golden brown.
Alternatively, to grill the burgers, brush them with a
little oil and cook under a preheated hot grill for about
3 minutes on each side, or until golden brown. Drain
on kitchen paper and serve in burger buns, with sliced
tomato and lettuce and garnished with alfalfa. Serve
with ketchup or chillied tomato chutney.

For goats' cheese & beetroot burgers, mix together
125 g (4 oz) raw grated beetroot and 250 g (8 oz)
soft goats' cheese with the grated carrot, breadcrumbs
and peanuts. Mix 4 tablespoons chopped parsley
into the mixture. Shape and cook the burgers as
above and serve in the buns with some good-quality
tomato ketchup.

braised lentils with gremolata

Serves **4**
Preparation time **5 minutes**
Cooking time **25 minutes**

50 g (2 oz) **butter**
1 **onion**, chopped
2 **celery sticks**, sliced
2 **carrots**, sliced
175 g (6 oz) **Puy lentils**,
 rinsed
600 ml (1 pint) **vegetable
 stock**
250 ml (8 fl oz) dry **white
 wine**
2 **bay leaves**
2 tablespoons chopped
 thyme
3 tablespoons **olive oil**
325 g (11 oz) **mushrooms**,
 sliced
salt and **pepper**

Gremolata
2 tablespoons chopped
 parsley
finely grated rind of **1 lemon**
2 **garlic cloves**, chopped

Melt the butter in a saucepan and fry the onion, celery and carrots for 3 minutes. Add the lentils, stock, wine, herbs and a little salt and pepper. Bring to the boil, then reduce the heat and simmer gently, uncovered, for about 20 minutes or until the lentils are tender.

Meanwhile, mix together the ingredients for the gremolata.

Heat the oil in a frying pan. Add the mushrooms and fry for about 2 minutes until golden. Season lightly with salt and pepper.

Ladle the lentils on to plates, top with the mushrooms and serve scattered with the gremolata.

For lentil-stuffed mushrooms with gammon & red wine, cook the onion, celery and carrots as above. Cut 2 gammon steaks, each about 125 g (4 oz), into strips and add to the pan. Cook for 4–5 minutes before adding the lentils, stock and 250 ml (8 fl oz) red wine. Add the herbs and seasoning and cook as above. Heat 3 tablespoons oil in a large frying pan and cook 4 large flat mushrooms for 2–3 minutes on each side until golden and soft. Pile the lentil mixture into the mushrooms and serve on a bed of salad leaves and sprinkled with the gremolata.

squash with red bean sauce

Serves **4**
Preparation time **10 minutes**
Cooking time **15 minutes**

600 ml (1 pint) **vegetable stock**
1 kg (2 lb) **mixed squash**, such as butternut and acorn, quartered and deseeded
125 g (4 oz) **baby spinach leaves**
rice, to serve

Sauce
4 tablespoons **olive oil**
4 **garlic cloves**, thinly sliced
1 **red pepper**, cored, deseeded and finely chopped
2 **tomatoes**, chopped
410 g (13½ oz) can **red kidney beans**, drained and rinsed
1–2 tablespoons **hot chilli sauce**
small handful of fresh **coriander leaves**, chopped
salt

Bring the stock to the boil in a large saucepan. Add the squash, reduce the heat and cover. Simmer gently for about 15 minutes or until the squash is just tender.

Meanwhile, to make the sauce, heat the oil in a frying pan, add the garlic and pepper and fry for 5 minutes, stirring frequently, until very soft. Add the tomatoes, red kidney beans, hot chilli sauce and a little salt and simmer for 5 minutes until pulpy. Set aside.

Drain the squash from the stock, reserving the stock, and return to the pan. Scatter over the spinach leaves, then cover and cook for about 1 minute until the spinach has wilted in the steam.

Pile the vegetables on to servings of rice. Stir 8 tablespoons of the reserved stock into the sauce with the coriander. Spoon over the vegetables and serve with boiled rice.

For stuffed squash with beans & cheese, halve and deseed 1 kg (2 lb) squash. Brush all over with olive oil and roast in a preheated oven, 200°C (400°F), Gas Mark 6, for 30 minutes. Make up the sauce as above. Rinse and drain 2 x 410 g (13½ oz) cans of mixed beans and add to the sauce. Pile the mixture into the roasted squash halves and top with 125 g (4 oz) grated Gruyère cheese. Return to the oven for 15 minutes until golden and bubbling.

falafel cakes

Serves **4**
Preparation time **10 minutes**
Cooking time **10 minutes**

410 g (13½ oz) can
  chickpeas, drained and
  rinsed
1 **onion**, roughly chopped
3 **garlic cloves**, roughly
  chopped
2 teaspoons **cumin seeds**
1 teaspoon mild **chilli powder**
2 tablespoons chopped **mint**
3 tablespoons chopped fresh
  coriander leaves, plus extra
  leaves to serve
50 g (2 oz) **fresh
  breadcrumbs**
oil, for shallow frying
salt and **pepper**

To serve
4 **pitta breads**
2 **little gem lettuces**, torn
  into pieces
minted cucumber and
  yogurt salad

Place the chickpeas in a food processor or blender with the onion, garlic, spices, herbs, breadcrumbs and a little salt and pepper. Blend briefly to make a chunky paste.

Take dessertspoonfuls of the mixture and flatten into cakes. Heat a 1 cm (½ inch) depth of oil in a frying pan and fry half the falafel for about 3 minutes, turning once until crisp and golden. Drain on kitchen paper and keep warm while cooking the remainder. Serve the falafel in warmed split pitta breads filled with torn little lettuce, coriander leaves and spoonfuls of minted cucumber and yogurt salad.

For lunchtime pittas, make the falafel mixture as above. Fill warm toasted pitta breads with the mixture, thinly sliced red onions and lots of fresh coriander leaves. Make a fresh-tasting raita by mixing 150 ml (¼ pint) natural yogurt with 1 teaspoon mint sauce and ⅛ cucumber finely chopped. Serve the pitta breads with the raita on the side.

sweet treats

scones with whipped cream

Makes **about 10**
Preparation time **10 minutes**
Cooking time **10 minutes**

250 g (8 oz) **plain flour**
1 teaspoon **cream of tartar**
½ teaspoon **bicarbonate**
 of soda
pinch of **salt**
50 g (2 oz) **butter**, chilled
 and diced
25 g (1 oz) **caster sugar**
125 ml (4 fl oz) **milk**
 (approximately), plus extra
 to glaze

To serve
butter or **whipped cream**
jam

Sift the flour, cream of tartar, bicarbonate of soda and salt into a mixing bowl and rub in the butter with your fingertips until the mixture resembles breadcrumbs. Stir in the sugar and add enough milk to mix to a soft dough.

Turn on to a floured surface, knead lightly and roll out to 2 cm (¾ inch) thick. Cut into 5 cm (2 inch) rounds. Place on a floured baking sheet and brush with milk.

Bake in a preheated oven, 220°C (425°F), Gas Mark 7, for 10 minutes. Transfer to a wire rack to cool. Serve with butter and jam or with whipped cream and jam.

For lavender-flavoured scones, place 125 ml (4 fl oz) milk in a small pan and add 2–3 lavender flowers. Bring to the boil, then immediately remove the pan from the heat and leave to cool. Use the milk to make the scones as above. Serve the warm scones with clotted cream and a black jam, such as blackberry or blackcurrant, to complement the flavour of the scones.

banoffi pie

Serves **6**
Preparation time **15 minutes**,
  plus chilling
Cooking time **10 minutes**

Base
250 g (8 oz) **digestive
  biscuits**
125 g (4 oz) **butter**

Filling
125 g (4 oz) **butter**
125 g (4 oz) **light muscovado
  sugar**
400 g (13 oz) can **condensed
  milk**
2 **bananas**
1 tablespoon **lemon juice**
250 ml (8 fl oz) **whipping
  cream**
25 g (1 oz) **chocolate
  shavings**

Crush the digestive biscuits in a clean plastic bag
with a rolling pin or wine bottle.

Melt the butter in a saucepan and stir in the crumbs.
Press the biscuit mix evenly over the base and sides
of a deep 20 cm (8 inch) round springform tin or
similar. Put in the refrigerator for 1 hour.

Make the filling. Put the butter and sugar in a
saucepan over a low heat. Once the butter has melted,
stir in the condensed milk and bring slowly to the boil.
Turn down the heat and simmer for 5 minutes, stirring
all the time, until the mixture turns a caramel colour.
Pour on to the biscuit base and chill in the refrigerator
for about 1 hour, until the mixture has set.

Slice the bananas and toss in the lemon juice. Keep
a quarter of the bananas for the top and spread the
rest over the filling.

Whip the cream until it forms soft peaks and spoon
it over the top. Decorate with the rest of the banana
slices and sprinkle with the chocolate shavings.

For extra-chocolate banoffi pie, make the base
with 250 g (8 oz) chocolate digestive biscuits and
125 g (4 oz) butter. Make the filling as above. Once
the cream has been softly whipped, melt 50 g (2 oz)
plain dark chocolate and pour it over the cream.
Use a metal spoon to swirl the chocolate carefully
into the cream to marble it. Spoon the cream over
the bananas and serve sprinkled with 25 g (1 oz)
chocolate shavings.

cranberry sponge puddings

Serves **4**

Preparation time **10 minutes**

Cooking time **25 minutes**

finely grated rind and juice of
  1 orange
150 g (5 oz) **fresh** or **frozen**
  cranberries
100 g (3½ oz) **caster sugar**
2 tablespoons **raspberry jam**
100 g (3½ oz) **butter**,
  softened
100 g (3½ oz) **self-raising**
  flour
2 **eggs**
oil, for oiling
custard, to serve

Put the orange juice into a saucepan with the cranberries and 1 tablespoon of the sugar and cook over a moderate heat for 5 minutes until the cranberries are just softened. Use a slotted spoon to drain and spoon half the cranberries into 4 individual 200 ml (7 fl oz) metal pudding moulds.

Add the jam to the remaining cranberries and cook for 1 minute until melted. Set the sauce aside.

Put the remaining sugar, butter, flour, eggs and orange rind into a bowl or food processor and beat until smooth. Spoon the sponge mixture into the moulds and level the surface. Cover loosely with pieces of oiled foil.

Cook the puddings in the top of a steamer or in a preheated oven, 180°C (350°F), Gas Mark 4, for 20 minutes until well risen. Loosen the edges with a round-bladed knife and turn out on to plates. Top with the cranberry sauce and serve with custard.

For double chocolate puddings, make the pudding mixture as above but omit the cranberry mixture. Replace the orange rind with 15 g (½ oz) cocoa powder. Spoon the mixture into 4 pudding moulds, then press 2 squares of plain dark chocolate into each, making sure they are completely covered by the pudding mixture. Cook as above and serve with white chocolate sauce.

chocolate biscuit cake

Makes **8 slices**
Preparation time **15 minutes**,
   plus cooling and chilling

300 g (10 oz) **plain
   chocolate**, broken into
   pieces
2 tablespoons **milk**
125 g (4 oz) **butter**, melted,
   plus extra for greasing
125 g (4 oz) **digestive
   biscuits**, lightly crushed
2 packets **white chocolate
   buttons**
2 packets **milk chocolate
   buttons**

Grease an 18 cm (7 inch) round cake tin or similar.
Put the plain chocolate and milk in a bowl set over a
pan of simmering water, making sure the bowl does
not touch the water, and leave until the chocolate has
melted, stirring occasionally. Stir in the butter. Remove
the bowl from the heat and leave until cool, but not
solid.

Mix the biscuit pieces with the white and milk
chocolate buttons, then stir the mixture into the melted
chocolate, pour it into the tin and squash it down
gently. Put in the refrigerator for at least 3 hours until
firm, then cut into wedges.

For fruity chocolate squares, melt the chocolate in
the milk as above. Chop 50 g (2 oz) glacé cherries
and roughly chop 50 g (2 oz) ready-to-eat dried
apricots. Combine these with 125 g (4 oz) raisins
and a small handful of mini marshmallows and mix
into the melted chocolate. Lightly crush the biscuits
and add to the mixture but omit the chocolate buttons.
Stir well, then press into a lightly greased 20 cm
(8 inch) square tin and chill for 1 hour. Remove from
the refrigerator and turn on to a board. Cut into small
squares to serve with coffee or larger pieces for a
teatime treat.

apricots with mascarpone

Serves **4**

Preparation time **5 minutes**

Cooking time **3 minutes**

2 pieces of **stem ginger in
 s rup**, drained and finely
 chopped

2 tablespoons **ginger syrup**
 from the jar

250 g (8 oz) **mascarpone
 cheese**

2 teaspoons **lemon juice**

50 g (2 oz) **unsalted butter**

25 g (1 oz) **light muscovado
 sugar**

400 g (13 oz) **apricots**, halved

3 tablespoons **Amaretto
 liqueur** or **brandy**

Mix the stem ginger with the ginger syrup, mascarpone
and lemon juice.

Melt the butter in a frying pan and add the sugar. Cook
for about 1 minute until the sugar has dissolved. Add
the apricots and fry quickly until lightly coloured but still
firm. Stir in the liqueur or brandy.

Spoon the mascarpone on to plates, top with the fruit
and juices and serve the dessert warm.

For pan-fried bananas with vanilla cream, beat
250 g (8 oz) mascarpone with $1/2$ teaspoon vanilla
extract and 2 tablespoons milk to make a smooth
cream. Transfer to a serving bowl. Melt 50 g (2 oz)
butter in a frying pan and stir in 25 g (1 oz) caster
sugar. Halve 4 bananas and cook in the butter as
above, adding 3 tablespoons of brandy, if liked.

quick tiramisu

Serves **4–6**
Preparation time **15 minutes**,
  plus chilling

5 tablespoons strong
  espresso coffee
75 g (3 oz) **dark muscovado
  sugar**
4 tablespoons **coffee liqueur**
  or 3 tablespoons **brandy**
75 g (3 oz) **sponge finger
  biscuits**, broken into large
  pieces
400 g (13 oz) good-quality
  ready-made custard
250 g (8 oz) **mascarpone
  cheese**
1 teaspoon **vanilla extract**
75 g (3 oz) **plain chocolate**,
  finely chopped
cocoa powder, for dusting

Mix the coffee with 2 tablespoons of the sugar and the liqueur or brandy in a medium bowl. Toss the sponge fingers in the mixture and turn into a serving dish, spooning over any excess liquid.

Beat together the custard, mascarpone and vanilla extract and spoon a third of the mixture over the biscuits. Sprinkle with the remaining sugar, then spoon over half the remaining custard. Scatter with half the chopped chocolate, then spread with the remaining custard and sprinkle with the remaining chopped chocolate.

Chill for about 1 hour until set. Serve dusted with cocoa powder.

For raspberry tiramisu, put 125 g (4 oz) raspberries in a pan with 1 tablespoon caster sugar and 2 tablespoons water. Bring to the boil, remove from the heat and beat with a wooden spoon to crush. Spoon into a sieve set over a bowl and press through the sieve to make a simple coulis. Prepare the other ingredients as above, omitting the coffee liqueur, and use the coulis to top the sponge fingers before layering the mascarpone and custard mixture. Add a layer of raspberries on top of the mascarpone. Sprinkle with cocoa to serve.

lemon & honeycomb pancakes

Serves **2**
Preparation time **6 minutes**
Cooking time **1–2 minutes**

125 ml (4 fl oz) **double cream**, plus extra to serve
40 g (1½ oz) **honeycomb** or **old-fashioned cinder toffee**, crumbled
1 teaspoon finely grated **lemon rind**
50 g (2 oz) **crystallized lemon peel**, finely chopped (optional)
80 ml (2½ fl oz) traditional **lemon curd**
6 **Scotch pancakes**
blueberries, to serve

Combine the cream, honeycomb or toffee, lemon rind, crystallized lemon peel, if using, and lemon curd in a bowl. Place a quarter of the lemon cream on a pancake, top with a second pancake and another quarter of the lemon cream on top, then finish with a third pancake. Repeat the process so that you have 2 triple-decker lemon pancakes.

Toast the pancake stacks in a sandwich grill for 1–2 minutes, or according to the manufacturer's instructions, until the outside pancakes are toasted and the lemon cream is beginning to ooze from the sides. Serve immediately with some blueberries.

For blueberry & honey layers, mix 200 ml (7 fl oz) crème fraîche with 1 teaspoon finely grated lemon rind. Make the pancakes as above. Spread lemon cream over a pancake, sprinkle over a few blueberries and drizzle over some honey. Continue the layering, finishing with a pancake. Drizzle with a little honey to serve.

instant apple crumbles

Serves **4**
Preparation time **7 minutes**
Cooking time **13 minutes**

1 kg (2 lb) **Bramley apples**,
  peeled, cored and thickly
  sliced
25 g (1 oz) **butter**
2 tablespoons **caster sugar**
1 tablespoon **lemon juice**
2 tablespoons **water**
cream or **ice cream**, to serve

Crumble

50 g (2 oz) **butter**
75 g (3 oz) **fresh wholemeal
  breadcrumbs**
25 g (1 oz) **pumpkin seeds**
2 tablespoons **soft brown
  sugar**

Place the apples in a saucepan with the butter, sugar,
lemon juice and measurement water. Cover and simmer
for 8–10 minutes, until softened.

Melt the butter for the crumble in a frying pan, add the
breadcrumbs and stir-fry until lightly golden, then add
the pumpkin seeds and stir-fry for a further 1 minute.
Remove from the heat and stir in the sugar.

Spoon the apple mixture into bowls, sprinkle with the
crumble and serve with cream or ice cream.

For instant pear & chocolate crumble, cook 1 kg
(2 lb) pears in the butter, sugar and water as above,
adding $^{1}/_{2}$ teaspoon ground ginger to the butter.
Prepare the crumble as above, replacing the pumpkin
seeds with 50 g (2 oz) roughly chopped plain
chocolate. Cook as above.

chocolate millefeuilles

Serves **4**
Preparation time **10 minutes**
Cooking time **10 minutes**

600 g (1 lb 3½ oz) **dark
chocolate**, melted
200 g (7 oz) **milk chocolate**,
melted
250 g (8 oz) **mascarpone
cheese**
100 g (3½ oz) **rasperries**
finely chopped **nuts**,
to decorate

Spread a thin layer of melted chocolate on to a sheet of baking parchment. Drizzle more melted chocolate in a contrasting colour over the top and feather the 2 chocolates together. Leave until set but not brittle.

Cut into 7 cm (3 inch) squares, then leave until brittle before peeling away the paper.

Layer the chocolate rectangles with spoonfuls of mascarpone and raspberries and sprinkle with some nuts to decorate.

For raspberry millefeuilles, use 800 g (1 lb 10 oz) white chocolate to make the squares as above. Layer with cream and raspberries. Make a coulis by mixing 125 g (4 oz) fresh raspberries with 1 teaspoon icing sugar. Press the mixture through a sieve. Drizzle the coulis around the millefeuilles before serving.

victoria sponge

Serves **8**
Preparation time **15 minutes**
Cooking time **20–25 minutes**

175 g (6 oz) **butter**, at room
  temperature, plus extra
  for greasing
175 g (6 oz) **caster sugar**
3 **eggs**
1 teaspoon **vanilla extract**
175 g (6 oz) **self-raising flour**
1 teaspoon **baking powder**
3 tablespoons **strawberry jam**
icing sugar, to decorate

Put the butter and sugar in a mixing bowl and beat together with a wooden spoon until pale and creamy. Gradually beat in the eggs and vanilla extract, a little at a time, adding 1 tablespoon of flour with each addition – this will help to prevent the mixture from curdling.

Sift the remaining flour and baking powder into the bowl and fold gently into the creamed mixture.

Divide the mixture between two lightly oiled 18 cm (7 inch) sandwich tins that have been lined with a circle of greaseproof paper or non-stick baking paper. Spread the tops level, then bake in a preheated oven at 180°C (350°F), Gas Mark 4, for about 20 minutes or until the cake will spring back when lightly pressed with a fingertip. Leave to cool for 5 minutes, then loosen and turn the cakes out on to a wire rack, peel off the lining paper and leave to cool.

Put one of the cakes, top downwards on to a serving plate, spread with the jam, then top with the second cake. Dust the top with sifted icing sugar and cut into slices to serve.

For coffee & walnut cake, dissolve 3 tablespoons instant coffee in 2 tablespoons boiling water. Fold into the sponge mixture and bake as above. Make a coffee buttercream by beating together 250 g (8 oz) icing sugar, 125 g (4 oz) softened unsalted butter and 1 teaspoon instant coffee dissolved in 1 teaspoon boiling water until well blended and smooth. When the cakes are cool, spread the buttercream between the layers and scatter over 50 g (2 oz) finely chopped walnuts. Dust with icing sugar before serving.

pears with chocolate crumble

Serves **4**

Preparation time **5 minutes**

Cooking time **8 minutes**

50 g (2 oz) **light muscovado sugar**

150 ml (¼ pint) **water**

25 g (1 oz) **raisins**

½ teaspoon **ground cinnamon**

4 ripe **dessert pears**, peeled, halved and cored

40 g (1½ oz) **unsalted butter**

50 g (2 oz) **porridge oats**

25 g (1 oz) **hazelnuts**, roughly chopped

50 g (2 oz) **plain chocolate** or **milk chocolate**, chopped

lightly **whipped cream** or **Greek yogurt**, to serve (optional)

Place half of the sugar in a frying pan or wide sauté pan with the measurement water and the raisins and cinnamon. Bring just to the boil, add the pears and simmer gently, uncovered, for about 5 minutes until the pears are slightly softened.

Melt the butter in a separate frying pan or saucepan. Add the porridge oats and fry gently for 2 minutes. Stir in the remaining sugar and cook over a gentle heat until golden.

Spoon the pears on to serving plates. Stir the hazelnuts and chocolate into the oats mixture. Once the chocolate starts to melt, spoon over the pears. Serve topped with whipped cream or Greek yogurt, if liked.

For pan-fried oranges with chocolate crumble,

use a serrated knife to cut the tops and bottoms from 4 oranges. Remove the rind and cut the oranges into thick slices. Heat 25 g (1 oz) butter in a frying pan, add half the sugar and orange slices and cook as above, omitting the water, raisins and cinnamon. Make the crumble as above. Serve the warm pan-fried oranges with the chocolate crumble scattered over them.

chocolate chip cookies

Makes **25**
Preparation time **10 minutes**
Cooking time **15–20 minutes**

125 g (4 oz) **butter**, softened,
  plus extra for greasing
50 g (2 oz) light **soft brown
  sugar**
1 **egg**, beaten
150 g (5 oz) **self-raising flour**
125 g (4 oz) **plain chocolate**,
  finely chopped

Grease a baking sheet lightly.

Put the butter and sugar in a mixing bowl and beat together with a wooden spoon until light and fluffy. Beat in the egg, then sift in the flour. Add the chocolate pieces and mix thoroughly.

Put 25 teaspoonfuls of the mixture slightly apart on the baking sheet and bake in a preheated oven, 180°C (350°F), Gas Mark 4, for 15–20 minutes until golden brown.

Remove from the oven and leave on the baking sheet for 1 minute, then transfer to a wire rack and leave to cool.

For oatmeal & raisin cookies, mix the butter and sugar as above. Add the egg and flour, replacing 25 g (1 oz) of the self-raising flour with 25 g (1 oz) porridge oats. Add 1 teaspoon mixed spice to the flour. Omit the chocolate but add 125 g (4 oz) juicy raisins. Shape and cook the dough as above and eat the cookies while they are still warm.

quick hazelnut melts

Makes **20**
Preparation time **10 minutes**
Cooking time **15 minutes**

50 g (2 oz) blanched
 hazelnuts
125 g (4 oz) **butter**, softened,
 plus extra for greasing
50 g (2 oz) **caster sugar**
150 g (5 oz) **plain flour**

Grind the hazelnuts in a food processor until fairly smooth, but still retaining a little texture. Dry-fry in a heavy-based frying pan over a low heat until evenly golden. Tip into a bowl and stir until cool.

Blend the butter and sugar together in the processor until creamy. Add the flour and cooled nuts and process again to make a soft dough.

Take walnut-size pieces of the dough and shape into rolls, then pat into flat ovals. Place on a greased baking sheet and bake in a preheated oven, 190°C (375°F), Gas Mark 5, for 12 minutes, until just golden. Cool on a wire rack.

For chocolate & hazelnut creams, make 20 small biscuits as above and leave to cool. Sandwich 2 biscuits together using 1 teaspoon of proprietary chocolate and hazelnut spread between each. Serve lightly dusted with a little cocoa for a real treat.

pineapple panettone sandwich

Serves **2**
Preparation time **4 minutes**
Cooking time **2–3 minutes**

4 **pineapple rings** in juice,
　drained
4 slices of **panettone**
15 g (½ oz) **mini
　marshmallows**
40 g (1½ oz) **macadamia
　nuts**, crushed
2 tablespoons **vanilla sugar**
icing sugar, sifted, to
　decorate

Pat the pineapple rings dry on kitchen paper and arrange them on 2 slices of panettone. Scatter with the marshmallows and crushed macadamia nuts and sprinkle with the vanilla sugar. Top with the remaining 2 slices of panettone.

Toast in a sandwich grill for 2–3 minutes, or according to the manufacturer's instructions, until the bread is golden and the marshmallows are beginning to melt. Slice each sandwich into small rectangles and dust with icing sugar. Serve immediately.

For apricot & ginger topped sandwiches, lightly grill one side of 4 slices of brioche. Drain 400 g (13 oz) canned apricot halves and arrange the apricots on the untoasted side of 2 brioche slices. Place the slices on a grill pan. Scatter over 40 g (1½ oz) crushed macadamia nuts and 1 finely chopped piece of stem ginger. Sprinkle over the sugar and top with the other slices of brioche, untoasted side up, and grill for 2–3 minutes. Serve as above.

chocolate puddle pudding

Serves **4–6**
Preparation time **15 minutes**
Cooking time **15 minutes**

75 g (3 oz) **unsalted butter**,
  at room temperature
75 g (3 oz) **light soft brown**
  sugar
3 **eggs**
65 g (2½ oz) **self-raising**
  flour
3 tablespoons **cocoa powder**
½ teaspoon **baking powder**
icing sugar, to decorate
ice cream or **cream**, to serve

Sauce
2 tablespoons **cocoa powder**
50 g (2 oz) **light soft**
  brown sugar
250 ml (8 fl oz) boiling **water**

Rub a little of the butter all over the base and sides of a cooking dish and stand the dish on a baking sheet. Put the butter, sugar and eggs in a large bowl and sift in the flour, cocoa powder and baking powder. Beat together with a wooden spoon until they form a smooth mixture. Spoon the pudding mixture into the dish and spread the top level.

Put the cocoa and sugar for the sauce into a small bowl and mix in a little of the measurement boiling water to make a smooth paste. Gradually mix in the rest of the water, then pour the cocoa sauce over the pudding mixture.

Bake in a preheated oven, 180°C (350°F), Gas Mark 4, for 15 minutes or until the sauce has sunk to the bottom of the dish and the pudding is well risen. Sift a little icing sugar over the pudding and serve with scoops of vanilla ice cream or a little pouring cream.

For individual puddle puddings with orange cream,
prepare the mixture as above and spoon it into 4 lightly greased ramekins. Bake as above for 10–12 minutes or until the puddings are well risen. Mix clotted cream with a little finely grated orange rind. Serve the warm puddings with a spoonful of the cream.

sabayon

Serves **4–6**
Preparation time **5 minutes**
Cooking time **5 minutes**

4 **egg yolks**
4 tablespoons **caster sugar**
100 ml (3½ fl oz) **dessert wine**
2 tablespoons **water**
thin shortbread biscuits, to serve

Put all the ingredients in a heatproof bowl. Rest the bowl over a saucepan of gently simmering water, making sure that the bowl doesn't touch the water.

Beat the mixture using a hand-held electric whisk or balloon whisk for about 5 minutes, until it is very thick and foamy – the whisk should leave a trail when it is lifted from the bowl.

Remove the bowl from the heat and whisk for a further 2 minutes. Spoon the sabayon into glasses or a warmed jug and serve immediately (it will collapse if left to stand) with thin shortbread biscuits.

For zabaglione, a classic Italian dessert, make as above but use Marsala in place of the dessert wine. Serve in glasses with cantuccini or biscotti to accompany.

index

238

239

acknowledgements

Executive Editor: Eleanor Maxfield
Senior Editor: Charlotte Macey
Executive Art Editor: Penny Stock
Designer: Barbara Zuniga
Photographer: Will Heap
Food Stylist: Sara Lewis
Prop Stylist: Rachel Jukes
Senior Production Controller: Carolin Stransky
Special Photography: © Octopus Publishing Group Limited/Will Heap

Other Photography: © Octopus Publishing Group/Stephen Conroy 12, 13, 43, 47, 51, 144, 221, 235; /David Jordan 53; /William Lingwood 29, 39, 119, 131, 167, 185, 205, 209, 227; /David Loftus 65; /David Munns 108; /Peter Myers 37; /Sean Myers 115, 135, 159, 175; /Lis Parsons 6, 10, 11, 54, 86, 176, 202, 217, 231; /William Reavell 69, 71, 127, 129, 165, 193, 199, 213, 225; /Simon Smith 19, 157; /Ian Wallace 16, 85, 121, 123, 137, 141, 229.